SUFFOLK
Villages

Harold Mills West

with photographs by Mark Mitchels

COUNTRYSIDE BOOK
Newbury, Berkshire

First published 2002
© Photographs – Mark Mitchels 2002
© Text – Harold Mills West 2002

COUNTRYSIDE BOOKS
3 Catherine Road
Newbury, Berkshire

To view our complete range of books,
please visit us at
www.countrysidebooks.co.uk

ISBN 1 85306 751 2

The front cover photograph is of Kersey
and the photograph on page 1 shows Rattlesden

Designed by Graham Whiteman

Typeset by Techniset Typesetters, Newton-le-Willows
Produced through MRM Associates Ltd., Reading
Printed in Italy

FOREWORD

These are the villages of my native Suffolk. Not every one is listed, since this is no guide or gazetteer but an affectionate summarising of some of those from which, I hope, a sense of the county's spirit and charm can be deduced.

It is a book of peep-holes, looking at people and places past and present and sometimes upon great events that have mingled with humble lives. It is also, I like to think, a wheedling and a cajoling book that will persuade the traveller that there is life beyond the dual-carriage highway and a special charm awaiting any who will turn aside into our quiet by-ways. If anyone can walk more than half a mile along our lanes without coming to a pleasant spot, a clump of trees, a pond or stream or just a gate to lean on, he will be very unlucky indeed. And if he ventures a little further he is bound to come to the church and hall, war memorial and public house of some village, a prospect immediately pleasant while yet being inextricably woven into the past. The threads of a rich tapestry are there for any who care to pick them up. I hope this book may tempt the reader to do so.

No doubt more recent arrivals in the county could explain their reasons for settling here. Perhaps it is the attraction of fine rivers or the long coastline; perhaps of great churches and village architecture; perhaps of heathland and forest or the sharp, clear winds from the sea. It could be something of all these things. It could also be because an air of innocence still lingers in our villages. After all, that is what most people are searching for.

Harold Mills West

The peacefulness of Chelsworth

⌘ ALDHAM

Aldham may not immediately set your blood racing with excitement. The houses, most of them substantial and independent-looking, straggle along the village street. Yet, if you have an hour to spare on a fine summer's afternoon, take the side road from the village that leads nowhere but to a farm and the church. The church is 'miles away' from the houses but in its vicinity is one of the pleasantest spots you could find in a day's journey. There are low, grazing meadows with a handful of sheep and the hint of a stream and a pond all lying close below the mound on which the round-towered church rests

Inside the church a wealth of timber stretches almost from floor to roof, so that the occasional visitor, like the regular worshipper, can bask in the warm glow of the polished wood, a welcome contrast to the cold plaster encountered all too often. Outside, footpaths will tempt you into the meadows to savour the balm of this completely tranquil place.

It was not always so. It was near by, on the Common, that the martyr, Dr Rowland Taylor, was brought to die a terrible death at the stake. He had been dragged from his church in Hadleigh on the orders of Mary Tudor. In the agony of that journey he recovered some momentary curiosity as to his whereabouts and was told he was upon Aldham Common. 'Well, thanks be to God,' he said, 'I am even at home.' A memorial is set there now with the words: 'Anno Domini 1555. Dr Taylor, for defending what was good, at this place lost his blood.' On a brass plate in Hadleigh church, the martyr is remembered as: 'An excellent Devyne and Doctor of the Civill Lawe. A preacher rare and fyne.'

⌘ ASPALL

Lord Kitchener was proud to add the name of this tiny village to his august titles – 'Viscount Kitchener of Khartoum in the Sudan, of the Vaal in South Africa and of Aspall in the county of Suffolk'.

It was at Aspall Hall that Kitchener's mother was born, a member of that family so long and so closely a part of local history – the Chevalliers. In 1845 Anne Frances Chevallier married Henry Kitchener, left the beautiful moated family house and in Ireland gave birth to the future military hero.

In Aspall, the Chevalliers conceived the extraordinary idea of setting up a cider press in the heart of Suffolk where there was scarcely an apple tree to be seen for miles. Even more extraordinary, they obviously hoped that it would be a commercial success though it has been suggested since that the only reason for the venture was the Chevalliers' own partiality for cider. Whatever the motive, they could scarcely have foreseen that the concern would still be going strong 250 years later.

Aspall cider – Chevallier barley. The synonyms are as familiar as any household names to local people and not unknown to those in far-flung climes. The story of Chevallier barley is told in the *History of Debenham* of 1845 and shows how a little luck and much patience and application can lead to far-reaching results. About the year 1880, we are told, a farm labourer by the name of John Andrews had been working all day at the threshing of barley. Walking home in the evening he felt some discomfort through the fact that some barley grains had worked their way into his boots. His first task on reaching home was to take his boots off and shake out the offending material. There was part of an ear of barley and several loose grains, all obviously from the same ear. Idly examining what had caused him so much discomfort, he soon realised that the grains were exceptionally large and well-shaped. John Andrews was a thoughtful and conscientious man to whom all aspects of arable farming were of interest. He kept the grains carefully until the spring and then planted them in his garden. There were only three or four shoots that came to an ear but by a further piece of good fortune they were noticed by John Chevallier when he came to the cottage. An enthusiastic agriculturalist, John Chevallier at once saw the possibilities in the situation and the nurturing of the precious seeds rested thenceforward in his hands. For several years the grain was sown over and over again until there was enough to sow an acre. From then on, it had only to be seen to be believed. Chevallier barley spread over the fields and over the county and out over many a field and county far removed from little Aspall.

⌘ ASSINGTON

Brampton Gurdon – which could well do for a place-name – was in fact the name of the most prominent member of that expansive seventeenth century family of Assington Hall, the Gurdons. His domestic achievements can still be seen in the church monument where he proudly poses with a wife on each side of him and beside each wife her considerable offspring, in total ten sons and six daughters.

With many other distinguished East Anglian families, the Gurdons chose to fight for Parliament during the Civil War and earned the personal gratitude of Oliver Cromwell, who came to Assington Hall during the siege of Colchester and made his headquarters there. Despite this association, the Gurdons apparently suffered no slight or retribution from the Royalists after the Restoration. Another domestic record was made by Brampton's eldest son who died in 1679 after 55 years of married bliss.

In August 1957, fire broke out at the Hall. When the brigade arrived the fire was well advanced and an inadequate water supply made the final catastrophe inevitable. The Hall was completely destroyed. A looker-on summed it all up in Suffolk style. 'That was a rare owd blaze,' he said.

⌘ BARHAM

William Kirby, the naturalist, was an incumbent here for 68 years. He was born a few miles away at Witnesham Hall and as a young man with Oxford behind him he walked one summer's evening to Barham to view the parish that was to be his. He found it 'a snug place for a young fellow to step into'. Snug indeed he must have concluded it to be since only the grave finally separated him from the village. Perhaps Kirby was the completely happy man – comfortably embowered in the insect-buzzing countryside of the 18th century and with the leisure to follow his abiding interest in observing all that was around him. He would surface from a study of some insect or plant only long enough to write a monograph for the Royal Society and then become absorbed again in the endless mysteries of instincts and behaviour in the creature world. In 1818 he was elected Honorary President of the newly-formed Entomology Society.

He was not the only one of the Kirby clan to attain distinction. As well known, perhaps, was John Kirby of Halesworth, the writer and topographer. His son John found fame as a painter and as a close friend of Thomas Gainsborough.

Not so fortunate in worldly affairs were the inmates of that Victorian house of gloom, the dark and forbidding-looking Barham workhouse. People have declared – such is the power of fiction – that it was in this very building that Oliver actually asked for more. There is no doubt that Dickens saw this workhouse when visiting Suffolk but probably he saw a great many others too as there was no shortage of such places at that time.

Social historians may well wonder at the juxtaposition of Barham workhouse with the vast estate and mansion just across the road known as Shrubland Park whose imposing gatehouses that hide the long drives to the house must be something like a mile apart. In earlier times this Palladian mansion was the home of the powerful Bacon family and then the Middletons. Sir William Middleton was an MP and High Sheriff of Suffolk. The Barham church provided for such importance by raising a front pew on four steps and ensuring that it was adequately cushioned and screened from the common gaze.

The handsome parish church stands upon the side of the hill encompassed with trees. Here the venerable old rector, Kirby, spent his happy years and there was a particular old cedar tree in whose shade he loved to sit and ponder on the wonders of the natural world. Not far beyond the church is Barham Manor, standing a little back from the road and for many years the home of the literary Hadfields. In the years after the war it was a delight to look through the gate and see peacocks strutting on the lawn.

⌘ BARROW

Barrow, or Barou as it was once called, was originally the property of the Crown. A thousand years ago it belonged to Edward the Confessor and was duly included in the Conqueror's possessions in the Domesday Book. Richard I made a wedding present of all Barrow's land and rights to the Earl of Pembroke on his marriage. Several changes of ownership followed until the 16th century, when the Heigham family took over.

Somehow the Heighams, whose name was taken from the nearby village of Higham, managed to secure respect from both sides during the religious differences of the Tudors. Sir Clement Heigham rallied to the cause of Queen Mary at her accession and was made Speaker of the House of Commons. In due course his son, Sir John, was just as energetic for Elizabeth when she acceded. When the Armada threatened, he was appointed to command a Suffolk band of infantry and a grateful Queen halted a progress through the countryside to visit him at Barrow Hall.

Around 1953 a howl of anguish went up when it was realised that the population of the 1900s had been reduced by a quarter and forecasts suggested that the village would stagnate. In fact, all such pessimism has been completely overturned by events, to such an extent that Barrow has been described in recent years as the liveliest village in Suffolk.

New houses and old make a good mix and the spacious green is a focal point for many of them. There is one house called the Gables but often referred to as the Doll's House which catches the eye simply because it is a tall, rather odd-shaped building with no known purpose in its design. On the edge of the village is Broom's Barn Farm, a 200-acre research station which has been devoted entirely to the study of sugar-beet, the only such centre in the country.

⌘ BARSHAM

There is a City here – strangely enough, for there is no street, no pub, not even a post office. There is, however, a row of cottages which earned this title at some point and the name stuck.

Barsham provides me with some of my earliest memories. There were hot summer days when we would walk down the long, sandy 'loke' to the mill and the river and we would lie on the footbridge to watch the clouds of minnows in the water and listen to the endless sighing of the rushes. The marshes beside the Waveney are never completely silent but are always mysterious and sometimes ghostly. Like all boys at that time I was irresistibly drawn to the clicking sound of a self-binder in the fields at harvest and would follow the machine as it went round and round the standing corn, throwing out the tied sheaves that would have to be stood up in 'shocks'.

The Sucklings, to whom there are many references in the village in one form or another, were lords of the manor. Famous above all of them is the name of Catherine Suckling, who was born at Barsham Rectory in 1725, the daughter of the Rev Maurice Suckling, for she was the mother of Nelson, the hero of Trafalgar.

Sir John Suckling has a place in the literary annals of the 17th century as the Poet Laureate, though this title gives only a sober picture of a man more distinguished as a warrior and – when there was no fighting to be done – as a gambler and notorious wild man of contemporary society. As often as not, Sir John was in conflict with the authorities over some indiscretion or other. On one occasion, after a particularly dubious series of adventures in Europe, he was hauled before the fearsome Court of the Star Chamber.

Somehow, he charmed himself out of that corner and was allowed to go free, one of the few to survive the experience. Afterwards, he retired for a time to settle quietly at Barsham Hall and write poetry. Among the more quotable of his lines are these:

> 'Out upon it, I have loved Three whole days together,
> And am like to love three more, If it prove fair weather.'

⌘ BENHALL

One of the surprises in the study of village life is the extent to which the gentry and lords of the manor looked after their own parishes.

Benhall: the leafy tranquillity of the Hall grounds

As far back as 1731, long before the arrival of compulsory state education in 1870, Sir Edward Duke left £1,000 for the education of the children of Benhall. Apparently a quarter of this sum was sufficient to build a school with a master's house alongside and to provide a playground and garden. The £750 remaining was invested and the income used to pay the schoolmaster to teach reading, writing and arithmetic to all the poor children of the parish. A hundred years later another benefactor, Edward Hollond of Benhall Lodge, updated the facility by leaving money to repair the school and to raise the teacher's salary. Soon after, another member of this family, the Rev E. Hollond, erected a National School on Benhall Green which was immediately attended by 60 boys and 55 girls – a very healthy number of voluntary pupils anxious to read and write.

Benhall Green lies a mile or so away, across the busy trunk road, and to take a short trip along the narrow lane to the Green is to sense a little of the old-style village life and this is repeated further on in the Sandy Lane of neighbouring Sternfield. Returning to Biggs Corner by the Sternfield road gives an excuse for a look at the church and its approach. This short, leafy avenue of oaks and beeches on one side and firs on the other makes a suitable introduction to the beautiful church mantled in trees and, in summer, with roses about the door. Beside the churchyard a plantation of poplars whisper above the peaceful graves.

⌘ BLUNDESTON

This village belongs to Suffolk and not Norfolk by the skin of its teeth and we duly

Blundeston churchyard

add the name to our many villages with literary associations. Modern pilgrims inspired by the printed word turn up at Blundeston from time to time, trying to identify some of the features described so memorably in David Copperfield. 'I was born at Blunderstone, in Suffolk,' David is made to say and later he speaks of the church with its high-backed pews where Peggotty tried to keep his attention from wandering during the sermon.

Happily, it is the sort of village which one can easily imagine could have seen the young David playing in the churchyard – 'there is nothing half so green as I know anywhere,' he declares later, 'as the grass of that churchyard; nothing so shady as its trees; nothing half so quiet as its tombstones.' It is the sort of place where Barkis becomes immediately credible and could be just around the corner urging 'the laziest horse in the world' to pull the carrier's cart. Miss Betsy Trotwood could come flurrying down the road at any time and present herself autocratically at the door of the old Rectory. Blundeston is content not to outgrow Dickens.

The village carries another rather tenuous literary thread, for the poet Gray used often to come to the Lodge here to visit his friend Norton Nicholls. Modern travellers are entertained well at the Plough Inn and can be forgiven if they avoid that large factory-like building not far away that is distinctly un-Dickensian and is in fact one of Britain's most up-to-date 'nicks'.

⌘ BLYTHBURGH

This is one of the great churches of the county, with an added power and beauty from its position overlooking the low-lying coastal flats – 'the cathedral of the marshes' it has been called. Rich merchants subscribed to the building of it and it forms an impressive monument to those who lived and traded here when Blythburgh flourished.

The town's wealth and importance came by way of the river Blyth. Shipbuilding went on here and a great deal of fishing. For a long time Blythburgh was undoubtedly a most prosperous town.

Now only the church remains to hint at the glory of long ago. Like nearby Dunwich, the town completely disappeared, not into the sea in this case but into decay and disuse. The life-blood of commerce that came by the river was halted when the river Blyth became choked and unnavigable.

Those merchants who knew Blythburgh well at its greatest and most prominent time must have turned in their graves when, early in the 19th century, it was decided to build a workhouse here, but this particular House of Industry inspired hate and resentment from the start. There was talk of prison-like conditions and harsh treatment of honest folk whose only crime was to be poor. On 5th August 1765, a gathering of several hundred men marched to the new workhouse intent on destroying it. Their plea was that they should be allowed to work in the fields and share the harvest payment as true countrymen rather than be taken over,

The rich interior of the church in Blythburgh

body and soul, by the Union. Soldiers were sent for to disperse the rioters and in a fierce battle one man was killed and six taken away to Ipswich gaol.

The incident had some effect on the authorities, for soon after, public assurances were given as to conditions in the workhouse. 'Good new Feather Beds will be provided,' it was promised. Also, married couples would have their own separate bedrooms but 'disorderly or Lewd persons will be punished by an Abatement of Diet'. The Victorians were ever masters of euphemism.

⌘ BOTESDALE

Botesdale – the dale of St Botolph – lies each side of the road about two thirds of the way from Bury St Edmunds to Diss. Houses and shops huddle close beside the long street which extends so far that at certain points not immediately obvious it runs into the territory of the neighbouring villages of Rickinghall Superior and Rickinghall Inferior.

A weekly market was allowed here during the Middle Ages and a fair to celebrate St Botolph's Day on the 18th May. Such excitements as this may have contributed to the profligate conduct of a young gentleman named Robert Bacon, of the wealthy and ubiquitous Bacon family, who became the classic bad egg, the bounder and cynic who boasted that he could scarcely wait to squander his promised inheritance. Some may have seen it as a well-deserved fate that he did not inherit at all, since he died before his father, perhaps of sheer ennui.

An earlier Bacon, Sir Nicholas, an undoubted goody of the family, obtained permission from Queen Elizabeth to build and maintain a grammar school here, an innovation well ahead of the times. The school flourished for over two centuries, providing suitable education for the sons of local gentry and farmers and turning out some distinguished characters including Hablet Browne (Phiz), the illustrator, and John Fenn, the publisher of the Paston Letters.

Three hundred and fifty years ago, mischievous young boys of the early school occupied odd moments in carving their names or initials on the beams. Some can be seen still. The oldest is that of William Swyer, aged eleven, who in 1609 gouged out for himself a name that he could never have imagined would still be read in the twenty-first century.

⌘ BRAMFIELD

Nowadays the busy A144 carries the majority of travellers summarily through Bramfield and onward the 3 miles or so to Halesworth but for those who pause here there is reward enough. Once there were two wonders to gaze at, but time has

Bramfield village

finally defeated the famous Bramfield Oak, believed to have been a thousand years old and a fair stripling when Alfred was king. It is spoken of in ancient rhymes; that ubiquitous queen, Elizabeth, sheltered under its branches and many a Suffolk cottager walked a few miles just to stare and wonder at the magnificent old tree. It held on to life with the grace and tenacity of an aged monarch and died with dignity, dropping its last three branches on a completely calm day in 1843.

The other phenomenon is still very visible – the round tower apparently belonging to the church of St Andrew but standing aloof some 20 feet away from the main building. The first impression that there might have been some aberration or mistake in the building of the church is soon dispelled. The tower was erected a century before the church at a time when powerful barons were at each other's throats and it was intended for defence, a modest fortress against possible attack. The only other disassociated church tower is at Beccles.

A remarkable epitaph adorns the gravestone here of Bridget Applethwaite, who died in 1737. It was someone undoubtedly of advanced feministic views who saw Bridget as something of a martyr who, 'after the fatigue of a married life, borne by her with incredible patience, and after the enjoyment of the glorious freedom of an early and unblemished widowhood, resolved to run the risk of a second marriage, but death forbade the banns.'

⌘ BRANDESTON

There was witchcraft at Brandeston, so it was said, in the 17th century. Matthew Hopkins, the witch-hunter, smelled it out immediately with his long nose. His accusing hand pointed to the frail old clergyman, a victim easy to subdue. The Rev John Lowes had officiated here in the 14th century church for fifty long years and, but for the hysteria about witches and the black arts, might have lived out his last few years in contentment. As it was, he became yet another sacrifice to ignorance and superstition. When he was accused of sending imps to do evil deeds he agreed that he had done so. At his trial at Bury St Edmunds he was found guilty and made to perform his own burial service. He was hanged there, with no one having the wit or the courage to protest, in 1646.

In contrast to this tale of misfortune there is the story of the remarkable career of another son of Brandeston. This was the famous lawyer, Charles Austin, the subject of open admiration by such distinguished figures as Macaulay and John Stuart Mill. He was born in 1799 at Creeting Mill. When his family moved to Brandeston, the boy's intellectual qualities were noted and he was sent to Norwich to learn to become a surgeon but his own inclination was more and more towards the study of law. In due course Austin became 'the first lawyer in England' and renowned for his oratory and conversational powers. For all that, having made a fortune and after refusing the post of Solicitor-General, he came back to Brandeston Hall to live quietly for the rest of his life.

⌘ BURES

Bures is practically the southernmost point of the county, and is a place predominantly of Saxon history. Somewhere nearby – the exact spot is a matter of debate – the young king Edmund was crowned on 25th December, AD 855.

At Smallbridge Hall, for long the residence of the Waldegrave family, Queen Elizabeth I was once entertained – at an unexpected expense, it seems, for the detailed items that made up the total of £250 were listed and later given to the British Museum.

Such events make history, no doubt, but it is at a lower level that we find the human interest. In this case it comes from the diary of a kind of peripatetic Excise man of the 18th century, a man who walked the villages hereabouts enforcing the laws on brewing. This particular officer seems to have been easy-going in the extreme for he speaks often of playing cards and feeling 'fuddled' from drink. When, at Ipswich in August 1786, he was ordered to go to Bures, he secured the high sum of six shillings for expenses and took four days on the journey. 'Dined at Lavenham,' he wrote, 'set out for Bures at one o'clock, got there at five. Found the Officer and wife very smart people like them much don't vastly like my quarters.'

It was not often that he held a good opinion of his colleagues. In September while still at Bures, he wrote: 'The supervisor came – don't half think he slighted me but don't care for him a rainy day hope he will get wet to the skin.'

His lodgings were far from being havens of rest for he complains – 'up all Night owing to Hop Pickers taking up the House.' Conviviality cost him a sore head on frequent occasions. 'Got fuddled,' he wrote in his diary, 'felt quite ill all Day.'

⌘ BUTLEY

The abbey at Butley was the most important in the county apart from the mother abbey at Bury St Edmunds. This priory of Augustinian canons was founded in 1171 by Ranulph de Glanville, who became Chief Justice of England. It was generously endowed by de Glanville during the period of his public success.

At the Dissolution of the Monasteries, Henry VIII disposed of the abbey to the Duke of Norfolk. In later times it became the property of Mr George Wright, who constructed the very handsome gatehouse using patterns of flint interspersed with Caen stone to pick out the detail of several coats of arms.

Butley stands on the edge of Suffolk's forest area, with one foot, so to speak, in woodland and bracken, the other on light agricultural land. Nearby are the Forestry Commission's soft-wood plantations screened by some of the more traditional of our trees, There are also some very ancient woods hereabouts, with hollies in particular estimated to be a thousand years old. Just as old, in fact, as the small Norman windows still discernible in the dignified and well cared-for parish church, the chancel of which was completed in the 14th century.

The Butley ferry

In spring the church is bedecked with daffodils, for here are the well-known daffodil woods. Every year I can remember people were allowed to go to the woods and collect a handful. When we were young we used to ride there on our cycles on the prescribed Sundays. With the sun shining through the trees on that carpet of gold, it was an excursion that held the very savour of spring.

⌘ CAVENDISH

It was the Gernons, a well-known and ambitious family with a seat here at Cavendish, who felt that they had practically everything except a good resounding name. Accordingly, they became the Cavendishes of Cavendish and forthwith impressed themselves as well as everyone else with their style. Distinguished as the Gernons had never been, they were soon rewarded with honours. John Cavendish, now a knight, was appointed Chief Justice of the King's Bench in the turbulent 14th century and served his king with zeal.

Sir John's undoing came with the Peasants' Revolt of 1381 and was caused by the unwitting action of his own son. It was a time of total unrest in the countryside and Suffolk rebels joined the revolt against old and unfair conditions of service. At Smithfield, as the history books tell us, the young King Richard II met the mob led by Wat Tyler, who made as if to draw his sword and was mortally wounded by a

The immaculate village of Cavendish

dagger thrust wielded by the Lord Mayor of London. Also by the king's side was John Cavendish, the Chief Justice's youngest son who, as esquire to the king, felt it his duty to despatch the rebel leader finally with his sword. His action brought the reward of an immediate honour for himself but a tragic end to his father. In Suffolk, the rebels ransacked the home of the Chief Justice before dragging him off to Bury St Edmunds, where he was summarily beheaded.

Such violence does not fit well with this most peaceful of villages. The whole atmosphere here, with the large green fringed with picturesque houses, is that of comfortable placidity. It goes without saying that Cavendish has several times won the Best Kept Village competition and is a little put out when it does not.

⌘ CHELSWORTH

It is now accepted as Chelsworth though given in *White's Suffolk* of 1844 as Chellesworth. This peaceful village with its half-timbered houses and placid open spaces is situated in the valley of the Brett where two small tributaries come together about five miles north of Hadleigh. Close by the church are the ruins of a very large mansion believed to have been the home of some very eminent person. The fields around are called the Park or Park Fields.

The painstaking work of an artistic monk from the medieval Abbey of St Edmund was discovered in the church about the middle of the last century and caused a local sensation. It was while some restoration work was being carried out on the chancel walls that a remarkable Doom painting was suddenly revealed. In the clearest detail it showed Christ on a rainbow with cherubs and angels in attendance but confronted by the figure of Satan, complete with horns and barbed tail and with flames all around.

Like most villages, Chelsworth has its memorial to the dead of the Great War, all the more admirable, perhaps, in that only one young man failed to return.

'The people of Chelsworth erected this tablet in proud memory of Charles Peck, who gave his life for his country in the Great War, 25th September, 1917, aged 19.'

⌘ CLARE

A thousand years and more of history have bestowed upon Clare a visible legacy from every separate age and created a kind of aura derived from the whole. It is not the ruined castle alone or the church or priory, nor the names and tombs of the famous that strike the visitor so much as the general atmosphere in which all these constituents seem to have been ingested long ago.

The stranger, however, has to view the parts separately and could not do better than to begin with the castle which is now enclosed within a country park. Not that there is a castle with any kind of entity but enough tell-tale signs litter the site to fire the imagination. It was of prodigious size and strength, built long before the Conqueror was born, probably during the Saxon heptarchy. It seems a remarkable fortress for the East Angles to find necessary in that area, for it covered some twenty acres.

With the coming of William I, Clare was made one of the 93 lordships in the county and it was given by the king to a relation, Richard Fitz Gilbert, for his aid at the battle of Hastings. Unfortunately, the line only continued for three or four generations before coming to a natural end without male issue. The estate was divided between three sisters, one of them Elizabeth, sometimes called the Lady of Clare. It was she who endowed and refounded the second oldest Cambridge college and called it Clare.

The church of St Peter and St Paul was originally built in the 13th century. From the majestic appearance of the church it is believed that it was erected by the lordly Clares and only later was permission given for commoners to use it. The nave was extended in the 15th century, the chancel altered in the 17th century and considerable changes were made in the last century. The result is this church of today that looks as proud as it is beautiful.

⌘ CLAYDON

Perhaps Claydon was always too well-placed for its own good. Even when a distance of four miles from the county town gave it some immunity from the urban spreading sickness, it was in the path of what transport then existed. The turnpikes that brought horse-drawn traffic from Bury St Edmunds and from Norwich joined together here in the centre of the village. Barges came up the Gipping to take lime and whiting from the factory and the river was joined by the railway when cement became the local industry.

No wonder that Claydon is now a focal point for roads going north and west from Ipswich and Felixstowe. A great roundabout with flyover now distributes fast-moving traffic to all points of the compass, while the old village hangs on in some stubborn loyalty to the past. Close by the roundabout is the lane leading to the old water mill that once made paper and afterwards took to grinding corn. There were many small cottages here and footpaths through meadows to the river. Where the roundabout now stands was an area of wet meadowland that for generations carried nothing more than osiers and masses of rosebay willow-herb.

Two coaching inns stand in the old centre of the village where a lane rises quite steeply to the 15th century church and to the farmhouse on the site of a moated castle. High on another hill, the centuries-old eyes of Mockbeggar Hall look down on lines of traffic passing through what was once its own private estate.

⌘ COCKFIELD

Surely there was never another village with so many Greens about it. Eastward of the Sudbury to Bury St Edmunds road, which at this point includes a good stretch of Roman origin, there is Oldhall Green, Cross Green, Great Green, Colchester Green, Thorpe Green, Almshouse Green, Buttons Green, Smithwood Green and Windsor. Together, they almost encircle the village.

Did Robert Louis Stevenson know all these Greens? Almost certainly he did. He knew and loved Cockfield and lived to be grateful to it for it was here that he found the encouragement for his literary career. Under the aegis of the vicar, Churchill Babington, who was a distinguished scholar and writer, R.L.S. met Sidney Colvin – a meeting that seemed to put a seal on both their careers. Colvin set the young writer on the road to success with practical help and advice as well as sincere faith in his ability and later in life was to complete his interest in R.L.S. by writing his biography.

There may be little here now that tells of Stevenson's visits but one can share the pleasure he must have had in this scattered, friendly village consisting of two ancient manors. One was Cockfield Hall which originally belonged to the Abbey of St Edmunds and was given to Sir William Spring after the Dissolution. The other, Earls Hall, was so named because it was owned by the Earls of Oxford. The estate was forfeited at one time because one of the Oxfords chose the wrong side in the Wars of the Roses but it was later restored.

This is in the heart of farming country. While the shade of R.L.S. may give us only a flimsy pretext for coming here, the charm and situation of the place confirms it as a good enough reason.

⌘ CODDENHAM

It was well over a hundred and fifty years ago when William Kirby, the naturalist, declared that the Spanish chestnut trees of Coddenham were the best to be seen in the whole county. Perhaps they are still. These majestic trees that grace the park that Nicholas Bacon devised provide oases of shade in the summer and successfully hide the Hall from the passer-by.

In Roman times the village was an important administration and transport centre. They built a fort beside where now the hump backed bridge straddles the soggy ditch of the river Gipping and they contrived to leave enough of their goods and chattels behind to inspire many an enthusiastic archaeological 'dig'. Perhaps the most rewarding of these was a 2,000 year old kiln which was unearthed in such perfect condition that it was fired again forthwith with complete success.

Since the beginning of the last century, the fortunes of the village have declined. A charming medley of picturesque cottages now house no more than 500 souls.

Coddenham

The old forge still exists as a recognisable shell that tells us a little of the days when there would be as many as ten horses waiting there to be shod.

Determined to see the famed alabaster carving in the church, I was a little taken aback to find it no more than a small framed artefact of about 18 inches by 12 inches. It depicts a crucifixion with angels holding chalices for the blood. The carving is almost priceless, I am told.

⌘ COVEHITHE

It looks strange and stark against the immense skyline of the Suffolk coast. Tall, jagged arches and tumbling walls sprout upwards in the ruins of an enormous medieval church and among the fallen masonry another tower of a later church, as if it were an abortive off-shoot of the other, joins the scene of desolation. It seems a rather dark and forbidding legacy for such a small, unassuming village that shelters alarmingly close to the encroaching sea. The forsaken tower looks all the more forlorn because of the faces and figures on walls and battlements, angels and grotesques together looking down as if reflecting on the futility of human effort.

Bilious Bale lived here when he was not following his argumentative path to power in the Church. John Bale – named 'Bilious' because of his ranting and nagging manner of speech – graduated from the Carmelite College at Norwich to go on to Oxford but came to the notice of Thomas Cromwell and under his patronage renounced for a time his career in the church in order to write morality plays. When Cromwell fell from favour, he himself felt it prudent to exile himself to Germany and like so many others became involved in the see-saw of Tudor religion. Returning to England on the accession of the young king Edward VI he was fully recompensed for his exile by being made a bishop but at the king's untimely death had to escape again from the vengeful clutches of Mary Tudor. It was not until Elizabeth followed her sister to the throne that he dared return, still inveighing against the tyranny of enforced religion but thankful to retire to the peace of the countryside.

⌘ DALHAM

The Kennet is no more than a rivulet here and wooden footbridges cross it at intervals in the charming village street. Famous men have walked here and two of them were of the name of Rhodes. Of the two brothers, the one that matters most hereabouts is not he who helped to found an Empire in Africa but his greatest ally and admirer, Francis, as great a patriot as Cecil and perhaps a greater man. Both lived here for a time since their grandfather owned the Hall and its estate but both followed their roving spirits and fulfilled their adventurous destinies in Africa. It was Francis who acknowledged his deep roots in his native village and though he

Dalham: famous men have walked here

died in Africa, only a short distance from where his famous brother already lay, he was brought back to the place he loved. He was only 54. Most of those years were spent in Africa as a loyal soldier, for he was present at Khartoum, at Ladysmith, took part in the Jameson Raid and was in the van of those who relieved Mafeking. At one time he was taken prisoner by the Boers and sentenced to death. After the war, still fascinated by Africa, he set out to explore and record the country from the Cape to the Zambesi but died before he could complete his self-imposed mission.

In Dalham, Francis had restored the church roof as a memorial to his brother and in turn a memorial was set up to recall the life of this outstanding man:

> 'Long travel in this churchyard ends
> A gentleman who knew not fear,
> A soldier, sportsman, prince of friends,
> A man men could but love, lies here.'

⌘ DARSHAM

For most of us who travel along the A12, the name of Darsham means one thing – a level crossing and a substantial but rather lonely-looking hotel at the side. This is

The village seen from All Saints' churchyard

the Stradbroke Arms and so far as the hasty traveller can see, the complete Darsham. It is something of a surprise and certainly a kind of reward for the effort, to find the very real village tucked away at the side. There is a scattered community of houses, many of them old-style with thatched roofs, in a pleasant association with the ancient church of All Saints.

It is no uncommon thing for those who build or repair large houses or churches and are proud of their work, to put a signature somewhere concealed until such time as later workmen may be required again. A few years ago the names of a carpenter and his mate were found in a window-frame of the Stradbroke Arms, pencilled signatures that survived within the woodwork for over a century. On 27th April 1859, the two men, A. Malting and J. Baker, bid for a kind of posterity and certainly succeeded.

During the same modernisation work it was found that the cellars had lengths of rail track for cross beams. No doubt the rails are part of the old line of the Southwold to Halesworth railway, which closed in 1929. There was something fabulous and completely comic about the Great Little Railway and it produced in passengers a feeling of enjoyment rather than irritation. A whole series of comic postcards of the railway remain as a reminder. Some show passengers getting off the train to pick flowers and the engine driver making tea, while on the platform old folk with long beards and covered with cobwebs from their long wait, survey the train with unbelieving eyes. I doubt if present-day rail travel in Suffolk could raise the same kind of a smile.

⌘ DENNINGTON

'The reason why I decided to come with you today', said my least favourite nephew, who knows everything, 'is because of the pyx.'

We were entering the porch of Dennington's magnificent church. 'Picks? Pics?' I asked, scratching my memory. For a stupid moment I thought it was a contraction of 'pictures'.

'Obviously,' said my nephew in his best know-all voice, 'I shall have to tell you what a pyx is. It is the ancient keeping place of the vessels of the Sacrament. This pyx is almost unique.'

It is certainly a rare find in a church. This cone-shaped cover was made in the 15th century and coloured red, green and gold. It hovers above the altar like a gigantic candle-snuffer. But my curiosity soon led me away to gaze at other treasures. For there is a wealth of ancient objects in the church and a wealth of background colour and ornamentation to set them off. Strange to think that at the end of the last war the church was in danger of becoming a ruin. Years of neglect, of village pennies going to help buy a Spitfire instead of into the offertory box, brought calls for action when peace-time conditions returned. A massive restoration plan was put into effect and the church stands now as rich and as proud as it ever was.

It would be a mistake to try and mention everything to be found in the interior since it would sound like a mere cataloguing of objects, but I remember in particular the elaborate carving in screens and in figures, on bench ends and roof beams. There is a long sand table on which children once learned to shape their letters, and an unusual Jacobean pulpit that is trebly useful, being not only pulpit but reading desk and clerk's desk all in one.

This is no shrinking violet of a church. It stands impressively within and yet somewhat above the community around. Just here the roads from many directions come together almost under the ancient walls and the tower seems to look down benignly on all who pass by.

⌘ DUNWICH

The merchants, shipowners and traders of the busy port of Dunwich must have known the earth was shifting beneath their feet even at the time of its greatest prosperity. A thousand years ago the coastline was gradually disappearing. Edward the Confessor had included a spit of land here in his tax survey that the compilers of the Domesday Book searched for in vain. The rich people who once lived and made their fortunes here could ignore the warnings for they were never urgent and, besides, no one was likely to get his feet wet in his own lifetime.

The shifting sands of Dunwich

Records of the reign of Edward I give some conception of the size of the port with a list of shipping that included 11 ships of war, 16 'fair' ships, 20 barks trading to Scandinavia and 24 fishing boats plying along the coast.

But the slow and insistent devastation was immense. In the middle of the 14th century a substantial part of Dunwich, including 400 houses, was lost. Soon after, the churches of St Leonard, St Martin and St Nicholas also disappeared. Two hundred years later the port was destroyed, the church of St John Baptist taken down and St Catherine had crumbled over the cliffs together with the chapels of St Francis and St Anthony. By 1715 the sea had reached the old market place, gathering the town hall, the gaol and all else in its path into its ever-hungry vastness. St Peter's church fell next and provided the local people with a particularly harrowing spectacle. As the churchyard was washed away the skeletons of those long buried could be seen in the sand below the cliffs.

All Saints was the last church of all to disappear. By 1919 a single stubborn buttress rested there until it was dragged away and later set up as a memorial to the lost town.

⌘ EARL SOHAM

I am afraid I spent quite a large part of my ignorant youth wondering what a shimmaker was. Nowadays there is no need to know. The shoemaker has gone

Earl Soham church enjoys a fine setting

with all the other tradesmen that somehow earned a living within a small community. In Earl Soham, admittedly a large village, there were five shimmakers at work half way through the last century. In addition there were these:

A thatcher	A bricklayer
A maltster	Two blacksmiths
A bricklayer	Two wood turners
A saddler	Two wheelwrights
A watchmaker	Two tailors
A glover	Five carpenters
A whip maker who was also a hairdresser	

On the other side of the counter there were few great spenders in the community. Two clergymen, two school teachers, a handful of independent gentlemen, a dozen farmers and an untold number of farm labourers seems few indeed to keep so many craftsmen busy.

The church has a fine setting at one end of the long main street and close to the old rectory and a cluster of substantial houses. Inside the church there is the warm welcome of polished wood and a cared-for atmosphere. Both chancel and nave reveal a wealth of carved figures. Here are creatures of all kinds from a fish to an elephant with one or two human figures and a camel with two heads.

With some reason, past rectors have lived out long lives here, serving this beautiful church and the village. In the 17th century Francis Folkes was rector for 54 years but this was exceeded later on by Francis Capper who stayed for 59 years. Richard Abbay made a comparatively hurried visit of only 48 years.

⌘ EAST BERGHOLT

This is a large and prestigious village only a mile or so from the main London road south-west of Ipswich and not much further from the broadening estuary of the Stour. It is generally regarded as John Constable's village and there is an atmosphere here still, despite the flocks of tourists and trippers, which can persuade one that there was something special here to inspire the painter.

Certainly he loved the place where he was born and his childhood was no doubt formative of the artistic eye. He would have been fascinated by the line and colour of old houses, of the beautiful church and the strange bell-tower in the churchyard. But most of all that was significant to the artist was the rural scene about Flatford Mill, just two miles away, with the broad sky and the calm fields of the Vale of Dedham.

East Bergholt – Constable's village

The church here in which Constable worshipped is a large and magnificent structure. There were three centuries in the making of it from the beginning in the 14th century. Inside, many of the fine furnishings have been contributed by well-to-do worshippers here. Notably, a screen to the lady chapel was given by Mr Mann in memory of 80 years of singing in the choir. He also added a screen to the chancel as a memento of his happy marriage. The lectern, too, is in thanksgiving for 40 years of married life enjoyed by another parishioner.

Perhaps the most unusual feature in the village is the wooden structure within the churchyard. It is a bell-cage, a building with an open lattice of beams in which are housed five great bells. They weigh over four tons and are rung by hand. They have remained in this odd bell-cage for 400 years, since they were put there temporarily, it was believed, while the tower was being completed.

⌘ EASTON

Everybody loves a crinkle-crankle wall. I don't know why but a straight wall is just a wall, while a crinkle-crankle wall is a joy forever. Its loveliness increases. One of the best and most undulating of such walls is here at Easton, where it surrounds the estate of Easton Park. The man who built the wall and the mansion it encloses was Anthony Wingfield, created a baronet in 1607 though not entirely because of the wall. The estate then passed to the Earls of Rochford until that line came to an end. It was taken over by the Duke of Hamilton who rarely graced the village with his presence, having vast estates also in Scotland.

The most notable of the less exalted families of Easton was Thomas Short. Against all sorts of difficulties he became a doctor in London at the time of the Restoration and lived to be hailed as a genius by some of his colleagues. Unfortunately, Thomas was a Catholic at an inappropriate moment for Catholics and the House of Lords made a great fuss and demanded his expulsion from the College of Physicians. It was to the great credit of that learned College that they refused to do anything of the kind.

Easton has a comfortable, tucked-up sort of atmosphere that is only slightly disturbed nowadays by the many visitors to the Farm Park, where old and new breeds of farm animals are on show to the public. The Earls of Rochford can never have foreseen such a thing happening on their private land.

⌘ ELVEDEN

Just before the traveller from the south reaches the Thetford Forest, he comes to the tiny village of Elveden. The busy A11 road passes close by but does not disturb the charm nor give an inkling of the surprise to be found here. For, despite the homely look of the woods and heathland, there is hidden away a touch of the exotic, a hint of another, distant continent. Even the war memorial makes such

The war memorial is 113 feet high

rustics as myself stop and stare. It is 113 feet high and forms an immense column that is hollow. Inside, there are 148 steps to the top which is surmounted by a great stone urn. The memorial reminds the passer-by of the sadness of war in general and of the men of Elveden, Eriswell and Icklingham in particular who did not return to the peace of Suffolk and their homes.

The magnificent Hall here, enclosed in a park behind ancient trees, discloses another unexpected sight – of a huge copper dome over a part of the building. It is a promise of the stranger features within – strange, that is, in the context of our quiet lives and undramatic countryside. For this was the home of the Maharajah Duleep Singh, an anglophile who retained many of the objects and customs of his own land but endeavoured to combine the best of both. His particular contribution to the house was the creation of what is called the Indian Hall, which is surmounted by that copper dome and supported by 28 columns. There are also huge doors covered by copper which has been richly decorated.

When he died, the Maharajah was buried here close by, leaving the Hall, the new church and the neighbourhood enriched by his sojourn here in a strange land.

⌘ ERWARTON

There is no village so small and unassuming that it cannot reveal some bizarre affairs in its past. At Erwarton, tucked away at the tip of the Shotley peninsula where the Stour and Orwell meet, a legend persists that the church here shelters the heart of a queen. And it is a famous queen, too, no other than the ill-fated Anne Boleyn who figures in this story.

Her association with Erwarton came when her aunt married one of the Calthorpes who held the manor here. The relationship brought Anne to stay in the village both before and after she became queen, apparently much taken by the peace of this quiet corner of the kingdom. When she met her unhappy fate, friends and sympathisers went to the place where her body lay and took the heart, bearing it with all respect to the church at Erwarton. Legend it could well be up to this point because there is no real evidence that this occurred, but as recently as 1837 a heart-shaped casket was found in the church during extensive renovations. It contained a handful of dust – perhaps the heart of a queen. Enough credence was given to the story to ensure that the casket was buried again in a vault beneath the organ.

In the Civil War, the village was a gathering place for stern loyalists who, on a notable occasion, fought bravely against a force of Roundheads until their ammunition ran out. With inspired ingenuity they took down the church bells and used the metal to continue the battle. Such are the legends of Erwarton.

The imposing gateway in Erwarton

⌘ FAKENHAM

This is Robert Bloomfield country. His mother was born here in a cottage opposite the church and probably told him the ghost story that he made the subject of a poem. Apparently a local woman was crossing Euston Park on her way home when she heard footsteps behind her. Frightened, she began to run but the footsteps followed just as quickly. When she reached the cottage door, almost fainting with terror, she looked round to see what hideous spectre was behind and found it was a young donkey that had lost its mother.

> 'No goblin he, no imp of sin,
> No crimes has ever known;
> They took the shaggy stranger in
> And reared him as their own.
>
> His little hoofs would rattle round
> Upon the cottage floor;
> The matron learned to love the sound
> That frightened her before.'

By chance another ghost story came to light in Fakenham in very recent years. Seven men employed by a London company to convert a row of four cottages into one residence met unexpected opposition to the work. According to the men, there were constant footsteps even when the floors were taken away. There were unexplained noises and sometimes there were pieces of plaster flying about. Their fright was so great that all seven men refused to enter the house again. There was much made of the affair by psychic sleuths determined to squeeze a ghost or two out of the story but like most tales of this kind it soon faded away. Perhaps if local country workers had been put in, the sort of men who know the tunes that old timber can play, it would have saved the ghost hunters a lot of time.

⌘ FARNHAM

The Farnham 'George' (now a private house) is the best-known landmark on this stretch of road between Wickham Market and Saxmundham. In front of its very door the road bends at almost a right angle and motorists are usually too busy negotiating the corner to take much note of the village. To be honest, there is very little there to notice – a number of houses around the former George inn and a church at the top of a short hill – but it is well worth the visit at the expense of a few minutes from the course of a journey. The flint church with its tower of brick stands on an eminence that could not have been better chosen for the view it gives. The ground slopes gently down to the river Alde, narrow but visible from here as is

Looking towards the church at Farnham

the restless A12 road, somehow out of keeping with this quiet place. The church of St Mary is simple and modest with high-backed pews.

The manor here originally belonged to Butley priory but came to the family of Glemham when religious houses were reduced. Sir Thomas Glemham was MP for Aldeburgh and a staunch, fighting Royalist in the Civil War. Sir Thomas secured the town of York for the king but had to acknowledge the gradually overpowering strength of the Ironsides. For his action on the king's side he was imprisoned at the end of the war. Later, he made his way to Holland to await the hoped-for Restoration but died before that came about.

⌘ FINNINGHAM

Prominent at every point in Finningham's past history is the name of Frere. In fact, a brass in the church records a whole list of them between 1736 and 1918 and as if this were not enough there are other monuments of other Freres from long before. The family came to settle here at the Hall in 1598. Since then many Freres have become rectors of the parish, others have been administrators and civil servants of high rank. In Sir Henry Bartle Frere, the village provided yet another of those characters that seem to have flourished on Suffolk soil, the kind that could quite equably combine a life of tranquillity at home with occasional forays into far-flung parts of the Empire.

Sir Henry's position in the Indian Civil Service somehow qualified him for a dangerous mission in Zanzibar at the height of the slave trade, and with due modesty he quickly produced a treaty in virtual settlement of the troubles and an end of slavery. But when Sir Henry was sent to South Africa during the Zulu risings he exceeded his brief and declared war on the tribes, for which he was suddenly recalled. The Empire received no further assistance from Sir Henry who never went abroad again but concerned himself with good causes at home.

Certainly the Frere family was good to the village. Eleanor Frere left a yearly sum of £12 to be taken from her estate and directed that it should be used in this way: £4 for teaching six poor children to read and write, £5 for providing coats for four poor men who were regular churchgoers, £2.5s for meat to be distributed, 15s for bread to be given out on the 12th of November. An earlier member of the family, Ann Frere, had left money for bread and for hempen shifts for the poor and for the teaching of four children.

⌘ FRAMLINGHAM

At the peak of the hill on which Framlingham stands is the great castle, a magnificent shell that hides the vacancy of its interior. Its origins are so old that it is simply assigned to the Saxon period. Perhaps the earliest drama that took place here was when Edmund, the young king of the East Angles, was besieged in the castle by the Danes until he escaped and made his way to Hoxne where he was recognised and murdered.

The most momentous year in the history of the 12th century castle was 1552. The young Edward VI had died and the country was split into two by the rival claims to the throne made by Mary Tudor and Lady Jane Grey. On July 10th Mary arrived at the castle, having proclaimed herself Queen rather prematurely since there was no certainty that she would be accepted. So finely balanced was the situation that Mary saw Framlingham both as a base and as a possible escape route to the Continent should affairs go against her. With great determination, she ordered county sheriffs and loyal peers to rally to her side. Rally they did, to the total extent of 40,000 men. Sir Henry Bedingfield brought 140 of his own men, fully armed and trained and was appointed Knight Marshal.

Mary, 'that demonical and blood-stained princess' as one authority describes her, stayed at the castle until the end of July before marching to London. There, she received a tumultuous welcome.

A hundred years later the castle was subjected to extensive Cromwellian demolition for the purpose of road-making. Today, like an aged monarch anxious to keep up appearances, the castle presents an impressive exterior to the world. As

Framlingham Castle

we walk over the solid span that was once a drawbridge and under the portcullis, it is up to us to rebuild the chapel and the other parts of the ancient edifice with the bricks of our imagination. At least they cannot mend the roads with those.

⌘ FRESSINGFIELD

The churchyard is as big as a park and no doubt well endowed with bones though there is only an occasional gravestone sticking up out of the grass. The church's exterior is massive but beautiful, 83 feet long and closely set with windows. The magnificent high porch was added to the church by Catherine de la Pole in the 15th century in memory of her husband and son, one killed at Harfleur and the other at Agincourt. Inside, there is a hammer-beam roof believed to be one of the best in Suffolk and there is much else that has survived since the church was built in the 14th century.

The village pump in Fressingfield

A story of the kind of which fairy tales are made has been recounted over and over again through the centuries. One day, we are told, the young prince who was to become Edward I was hunting near Framlingham when, after a heated chase, he found himself near Whittingham Hall and called there for shelter and sustenance. There he saw Margaret, the beautiful daughter of the house, and was so enamoured that he stayed at the Hall until angrily recalled by his father. The prince sought to protect his interests with the maid by asking the Earl of Lincoln to stay and guard her, for there were others seeking to ingratiate themselves. Two knights, one of Cratfield and the other of Laxfield, were already in love with Margaret and decided to settle their rivalry by a duel. By unhappy chance they were both mortally wounded. The way was now open for the prince to pursue his courtship but he was urgently required elsewhere and could not return to Whittingham Hall for some time, during which period Margaret, perhaps bemused by the excessive drama of so many suitors, decided to end the matter by marrying the Earl of Lincoln.

⌘ GLEMSFORD

One of the largest villages in what used to be designated West Suffolk, Glemsford spreads itself handsomely between the Stour to the south and the wandering Glem to the east. Its size and prosperity has been due chiefly to the successful silk and wool weaving industry.

The ancient records of the village go back a thousand years to the reign of Edward the Confessor, when the See of Ely held most of the land here and set up a college of priests. With all the immense privileges granted to it, the college flourished throughout the Middle Ages. In the Domesday Book it shows that Odo, Earl of Champagne, held the manor at that time.

Inside the church of St Mary is an oak reredos in memory of George Coldham, who was vicar here for 54 years, but one can look in vain for mention of George Cavendish, who was buried here. Cavendish was the perfect gentleman's gentleman to no less a personage than Thomas Wolsey. No mere servant he, for he was usher, valet, confidant, friend and ultimately biographer. He accompanied the Cardinal in all the pomp and power of great events and as a faithful ally he shared the ignominy of disgrace. He had given up all to join the Cardinal when, at the age of 26, he left wife, children and home to assume the role he believed he was destined to fill.

When the Cardinal was seized in 1529 and shortly afterwards died, Cavendish was brought before a council of inquisitors perhaps frustrated that they had not had the opportunity to grill his master. He was examined and cross-examined with great hostility as to the life, habits and conversations of the Cardinal but in his honesty showed himself to be only a loyal servant and friend without knowledge or interest in state affairs. Cavendish was acquitted and retired to Glemsford to write his impressive biography.

⌘ GROTON

As stiff-necked himself as the church that drove him and his like away, John Winthrop lived to introduce as narrow a conception of religion in America as he had renounced in England. He was born here at Groton in the year that the Armada sailed into the Channel, the son of the first lord of the manor after the Dissolution of the Monasteries had dispossessed the Abbey of Bury St Edmunds. John grew up to be a chest-beating religious zealot with the strict views of a John Bunyan. For all that, he rejected the opportunity to enter the church and became a lawyer, worldly enough to be a very successful one and to marry four times. There were fifteen children, doubtless all well-indoctrinated with fire-and-brimstone theology.

Religious persecution had already driven the Pilgrim Fathers to seek a new land and Winthrop was only one of 20,000 who about that time braved the Atlantic in their small, storm-tossed ships. However, some quality in John Winthrop earned him the post of first Governor of Massachusetts and he held on to this until his death in 1649. His government was stern and unequivocally concerned with his own concept of godliness and righteous behaviour. Soon after his appointment, a religious covenant was drawn up ensuring that only church members would be entitled to civil rights.

Winthrop, an outright Puritan if ever there was one, abolished all signs of frivolity as well as clothing fripperies such as lace. He regarded the days of the week and the names of months as idolatrous and made sure his followers were as much afflicted with sackcloth and ashes as he was. Just the same, he worked hard with his hands and was one of the most successful of the new colonists in setting Massachusetts upon the path of prosperity.

⌘ GRUNDISBURGH

The charm of this village lies in its well-arranged compactness. It opens up to the stranger with an immediate identity that usually persuades him that he must stop and look around. A good decision, this, for here is the centrepiece of the green and all around it, spread idly from different periods of the past, are church and shop, school and public house, besides a sprinkling of houses. The school dominates, having a superior position overlooking the green where wooden footbridges cross the infant river Finn and the visitor is lured to the shady cedars beside the church. There is a seat and a war memorial showing that seven Grundisburgh men earned military honours during the war.

The village green in Grundisburgh

Of the local craftsmen, the basket-maker survived longest. The Pipe family used their special skills for generations and I can remember very clearly how every week they used to drive a horse and cart loaded with clean, strong baskets of all kinds to the market at Woodbridge.

The church hides itself a little among the trees, perhaps embarrassed that its original tower fell and had to be built again in 1731. It is light and spacious inside and the eyes are lifted at once to the magnificent double hammer-beam roof of the nave, where whole rows of angels look down.

Along one of the narrow roads of the village is the large Baptist chapel that was extended in the 19th century to seat a thousand people. With two ministers, the chapel served those of a Non-conformist persuasion.

⌘ HAWSTEAD

There was some doubt afterwards as to whether Queen Elizabeth was much amused by the follies set out for her at Hawstead Place on her visit in 1575. One of them, apparently, was a gross figure of Hercules in the water garden 'which discharged by the natural passage a continual stream of water into a stone basin.' A distinguished rector of Hawstead, Sir John Cullum, later gave it as his opinion that 'modern times would scarcely devise such a piece of sculpture as an amusing spectacle for a virgin princess.'

The manor of Hawstead came to the Drurys in 1504 and the family left its mark on many aspects of social history before the line came to an end. Sir Robert Drury was elected Speaker in 1495 and in 1501 he obtained permission from the Pope to build a private chapel because the mile-long road to the parish church was 'subject to inundations and other perils.' One of his sons, Sir William, built the massive Drury House in London which gave the name to the adjacent Drury Lane. His brother, Dru Drury, was an Elizabethan courtier sent to Fotheringhay Castle to keep Mary, Queen of Scots, in custody.

An alabaster monument in the church commemorates the tragic death of Elizabeth Drury at only 16, a beautiful girl loved by a prince and also loved, to judge from his grief, by the poet John Donne. He saw in Elizabeth's death all the frailty and impotence of mankind.

> 'Her pure and eloquent blood
> Spoke in her cheeks and so distinctly wrought
> That one might almost say her body thought.'

⌘ HENGRAVE

The lord of the manor had a Lancashire accent and a background of trade but his pockets were full of good English gold. He was Thomas Kytson, soon to be a knight, a merchant who dealt in expensive materials like satin, lace and velvet in a constant trade with Flanders. He made his fortune shrewdly but spent it lavishly, settling at Hengrave in the 16th century having created the stunning magnificence of the Hall, which was 13 years in the making.

Sir Thomas lies now in the more modest proportions of the parish church nearby but even now impresses the stranger with the great alabaster monument which seems almost to fill the chancel. There are other tombs too, to the Darcys and the Gages. At the time that the manor belonged to Lord Darcy, it happened that his beautiful second daughter was pursued by three equally eligible young suitors. They were Sir George Trenchard, Sir John Gage and Sir William Hervey. Between them they made the girl's life an agony of indecision and on being importuned for the hundredth time she declared that she would marry them all. This in fact she did in that order as one after another died.

By her second marriage the manor came into the possession of the Gages. Sir John occupied himself mainly in writing a full history of Hengrave but he is also generally give the credit for introducing that succulent fruit, the greengage.

⌘ HEVENINGHAM

The reason that most people had for going to Heveningham was to see the Hall. On

Heveningham Hall gardens are an oasis

prescribed open days a fair number of us would climb into our cars, solve with varying success the enigma of exactly where Heveningham was and indulge our curiosity about the great house and its grounds.

The Hall is now in private hands but on a hot day the park itself is oasis enough and so spacious that a complete village could be enclosed there within its 600 acres. The Hall overlooks the park with great dignity, revealing Corinthian columns and an extended façade. It was begun in 1778 by Sir Gerrard Vanneck of the noble family of Huntingfield and finished in what is regarded as a better style by Mr James Wyatt.

More extraordinary was the ancient hall which the present one replaces. It was situated in a different part of the park and consisted chiefly of an immense central hall built around six great oaks. These living trees helped to support the roof as the branches grew upward and were also very convenient for the hanging-up of crossbows, hunting horns and other bric-a-brac of the time.

Throughout their occupation of the Hall, the Huntingfields have continued their interest in tree planting and maintenance and the entire area is impressively wooded with new and aged hardwoods of every kind. A famous tree here was the Queen's Oak, from whose shelter Queen Elizabeth I is credited with having shot a buck. The oak was almost eleven yards in circumference.

⌘ HINTLESHAM

Half way along the winding road between Ipswich and Hadleigh is the pleasant small village of Hintlesham, with its flint-towered church standing close beside the highway. Beside the road is the tree-flanked gateway to the Elizabethan mansion of Hintlesham Hall. It has a beautiful, chaste-looking façade and high Tudor chimneys and was built by the Timperleys who occupied it until 1740. There are many memorials in the church which point to the virtues and valour of this family. One monument on the north wall is to Captayne John Timperley who was killed in 1629 and it displays all the equipment and arms of a soldier of that time. It was erected by his wife, who declared: 'this memoriall is too too little to express either his deserte or her affection'.

Early last century the village knew well the figure of Havelock Ellis as he walked the lanes nearby. Though he had started life as a ship's boy, since his father was a sea-captain, he rejected the prospect of becoming a mariner after a particularly long and galling voyage to Australia in the 1870s. Back on land, he dedicated his energies to writing on the subjects of sex and psychology, creating a good deal of controversy as he did so. He died here in 1939.

⌘ HITCHAM

This is a large and straggling village about equidistant from Hadleigh and

Hintlesham Hall, now a restaurant, with an international reputation

Stowmarket. It is John Stevens Henslow's village as surely as Selborne is Gilbert White's. Henslow was rector here for about twenty years in the 19th century and brought enlightenment, scientific curiosity as well as fame to this backward community which at first had only contempt and resentment for the new parson. Had they known that he was Professor of Botany at Cambridge University and lectured to learned societies it would have made no difference.

Poverty was obviously the first difficulty, then lack of education, then lack of independence – Henslow tackled everything from the beginning, arranging thrift clubs, building a school for parents as well as children, planning ploughing matches and trying to secure land for allotments. There was outraged opposition to all. As soon as the school was established, the professor organised special classes in botany for the village children, an idea so successful it was later taken up by education authorities all over the country.

Soon, he began his famous botanical excursions, first with children to areas where collections could be made and plants examined. Later, parents and farmers and all would join the expeditions. The climax of these outings was the one when nearly 300 people went from the village to Cambridge and Henslow explained the work he was doing there.

⌘ HOLLESLEY

The church stands beside the tiny village centre in what seems to be a piece of wasteland. It has no porch but the arrangement of large flints and stone-work make the exterior walls look very handsome. It is worth the visit in order to see the great variety of carvings on the pew-ends, the most elaborate I have seen. They are chiefly of animals and birds, many of them of devilish aspect with tails and claws occupied in attacking and gouging their prey. There is a sciapod on its back with its huge foot over its head and there are also peaceful cameos of harvest scenes.

Nearby are a few modern houses mingling with the old and sharing the keen air that blows here across the open marshes by the sea. Just outside the village is the long-established Hollesley Bay Colony, to use its original name. It is now a prison. The rather bleak landscape here is given over to crops and orchards that are maintained by the inmates. As early as 1900 there was what was called a Colonial College here. In the *Illustrated London News* of 1905 is a description of the College where the unemployed were sent to be trained for farmwork at home and abroad. At that time there was much encouragement for single men to emigrate to Canada or Australia.

Close by is the road that leads across the open marshes to Shingle Street and the sea. It is a corner of the coast that has never changed – just an expanse of shingle beach on which a handful of houses stand, with a Martello tower for company. The houses still seem to cower from the winter's gales even in the summer. Overhead the curlews call across the lonely marshes and beside the single road the bullrushes are forever whispering.

⌘ HONINGTON

Pastoral poets around here would have their musings sadly interrupted nowadays by the sound of aeroplanes belonging to the nearby base but in the 18th century Honington was a hamlet of tranquillity and charm. Some of that atmosphere, as of being half-forgotten in these rural backwaters, still lingers among the lanes here and it is possible to imagine what it was like for Robert Bloomfield, the peasant-poet who was born in 1766. His early, formative years were spent here and though he was destined to leave the village it was always of Honington and its neighbourhood that he wrote, perhaps all the more poignantly because of his exile.

His mother kept a small school in Honington but the large family was poor and it seemed expedient to send Robert to join his brother in London and become a shoemaker. There he shared a garret with several other apprentices but somehow managed to write his best-known work, *The Farmer's Boy*, after the emotional experience of returning to his native village for a spell in 1786.

With the success of his poems, the Duke of Grafton became his patron and found him a comfortable job in the Office of Seals. After a time, bored and unhappy, with none too robust health, he returned to work as a shoemaker, tried the book trade and became a bankrupt. He died in poverty in a village of Bedfordshire.

There is a modest memorial in the church, fitting for this unassuming countryman who was also the very voice of our native fields.

⌘ HOXNE

Here was the martyrdom of the young hero-king, Edmund. He was crowned when only 15 years old and was pious yet brave, forever sought peace and found no triumph in victory over an enemy. In AD 870 the Danes were pressing forward across East Anglia despite King Edmund's efforts towards peace and at Thetford a battle became inevitable. At length the Danes prevailed, Edmund was driven back to Hoxne where he attempted to re-group his followers but, seeing that there would only be more blood spilt, he finally gave in and was taken prisoner. Perhaps, being magnanimous himself, he hoped that the Danes would prove likewise but they demanded terms in exchange for his life. He would have to yield up half of his kingdom, he would occupy the throne merely as a puppet of the Danes and he would have to renounce his faith.

When King Edmund refused, he was bound to an oak tree, whipped and relentlessly attacked with arrows. At the end his head was struck off and thrown down among the bushes. Legend comes in here with the carrying off of the head by a wolf and later, when the body was disinterred, it returns with the story that the head had become miraculously rejoined. A rough chapel of sawn trees and thatch was built over the grave and he lay there where he had fallen for 33 years before being removed to the town which was to become Bury St Edmunds. A cell of the Benedictines was established later on this site with seven monks and a prior dedicated to prayer for St Edmund, king and martyr.

Hoxne has a special charm in its situation here beside the Waveney where the little Dove joins in. The village is only a few miles from Eye and Diss but manages to retain a genuine rural atmosphere with its quiet lanes and interesting old houses.

The rural charm of Hoxne

Flax growing and milling was once much encouraged here and a mill on the Waveney that had been doing service as a corn mill was at one time converted for dealing with the more profitable flax.

⌘ ICKLINGHAM

The joint parishes of St James and All Saints form the community of Icklingham, which ranges for about a mile on the north side of the Lark. Here was an important Roman settlement and the two churches have been used from time to time to house the abundance of bricks and tiles and other remains which have been ploughed up in nearby fields. The bricks particularly are of much interest because of their great variety in shape and pattern, some with rough tracings of animals and flowers and some obviously having been vitrified. Apparently the settlement extended for about half a mile, most of it beside the river. There is a visible 25-acre square called Kentfield which some say is a corruption of Campfield. Coins, kitchen utensils and a lead cistern large enough to contain 16 gallons of water have been found here.

The two churches are about half a mile apart, with towers of flint where gargoyles, particularly on St James', leer down as you enter. All Saints' is the older church, with some recognisable Norman remains in the 14th century edifice and it contains much of interest including an ancient metal-bound chest and what was once a three-decker pulpit.

⌘ ICKWORTH

Although Ickworth Hall is now one of the showpieces of Suffolk, there was a time during the building of it when it was abandoned and it threatened to become a ruin. The many visitors to the Hall can feel satisfaction that the project was eventually completed for here is a striking piece of architecture of fairly recent times. It consists chiefly of a large, oval centrepiece which is capped by a dome which carries the height to 100 feet. There are classical references in its style, with columns of Ionic and Corinthian design and there are friezes carrying in relief the stories of the Iliad and Odyssey.

The ancient family of Herveys live here, its head no longer generally known by that name but as the Marquis of Bristol. The estate came to the Herveys by way of marriage. John Hervey was created a peer in 1703 by Queen Anne at the insistence of the Duchess of Marlborough and in 1714 he became the Earl of Bristol.

Ickworth Hall, one of the showpieces of Suffolk

In the 18th century the Earl of Bristol was a great art collector and an admirer of Italy. As a consequence, he was inclined to spend long sojourns in that country while at the same time he was beginning the project at Ickworth with the object of having a great house as a repository for his works of art. Unfortunately, the Earl's collection abroad was taken by the French in 1798 and he was confined for a time in an Italian prison. Such events upset the Earl's plans and he apparently abandoned Ickworth to its fate and spent the rest of his life in Italy. He died in 1803, having disposed of his remaining works of art apparently to strangers.

⌘ KEDINGTON

From long usage the name of Kedington has been reduced to Ketton in local speech, much to the dismay of those who see Kedington as a very special place. Lavish admiration has been bestowed, not so much upon the village but upon the great church. Someone once called it the 'Westminster Abbey of Suffolk'. 'The most beautiful church in any county in England', declared Sir Alfred Munnings. Other people, to be fair to rival churches, have found the edifice 'gloomy' and 'uninspiring'.

The church register dates from 1654 and the chancel is 14th century with the nave probably a hundred years later. There is a magnificently ornate 'squire's pew' and a three-decker pulpit but the interior is dominated by the monuments and inscriptions to the Barnardiston family, who were lords of the manor, squires and landowners for as long as history can recall. Certainly they were here long before the church and indeed they had a hand in the building of it. It is believed that there were Barnardistons in Kedington before the Norman Conquest. Through the centuries other Barnardistons have been added to the family vault. Last of all was Sophia who died in 1855.

The Barnardistons were against the king in the Civil War but changed with some alacrity at the Restoration in 1660 when Samuel Barnardiston gave such assistance to the king as to earn himself an immediate knighthood. It was Samuel, in his youth, whom Queen Henrietta saw from her window in the early days of the conflict and remarked: 'See what a handsome round head he has.' This is said to be the origin of the term 'Roundheads' for the Parliamentary forces but it could equally well have come from Captain David Lyde's scathing comment that they were 'round-headed, crop-eared knaves'.

⌘ KELSALE

Half a mile away the cars chase each other's tails along the A12 towards Lowestoft and Yarmouth. Yet here, Kelsale somehow drops an invisible curtain on the world of today and carries on as it always did. The old Guildhall dominates the tiny village centre; once it was a school and before that a shelter for paupers.

Wander a little further and there are small bridges over almost non-existent streams that lead past close-grouped rows of charming houses to a short, steep hill. Here, in a commanding position on the grassy mound, is the church, quiet and tree-sheltered and introduced by way of a lych-gate of magnificent size and construction. Faces and creatures look down from the battlements of the tower and below there are still two Norman arches over doorways. William Dowsing paid a visit here and recorded: 'We brake down 6 superstitious Pictures and took up 12 Popish inscriptions in brass; and gave orders to level the chancel and taking down a cross.'

The village has been well cared-for in the past, with great concern for the poor and for the education of its children long before schooling became compulsory. An amalgamation of charities provided money for apprentices and even for scholars to

The lych-gate of Kelsale church

go to university. From these funds a schoolmaster was paid £50 a year to teach 90 boys. He was also required to teach Sunday School but was provided with a house and garden, should he ever have the leisure to work on it.

⌘ KERSEY

Pride of place is a fine virtue when tempered with moderation. Too much of it can turn a village that is simply picturesque into self-conscious preciousness. Eulogies of praise and admiration have been showered upon the beauties of Kersey. It has the burden of being frequently elected the prettiest village of England. Indeed, when Lord Woodbridge opened the new village hall after the Second World War he felt that such a description was limiting and declared that it was the prettiest village in the world.

Because of such high approbation, residents naturally feel a special kind of responsibility for the general appearance of the village. There was the awkward invention of electricity, for instance. For most villages it was something that was welcome and overdue. For Kersey it was the sound of doom. If people did not actually tremble in their beds at the prospect of poles and wires in the street, that is certainly the impression that the stranger must get, knowing that an emotional conflict went on for fifteen years.

When at last electricity came to Kersey in 1949, it arrived with a ballyhoo similar to that at the switching-on of Blackpool's illuminations. In Kersey only 20 houses were to benefit but there were crowds to cheer the official lighting-up and a great banner that said: 'This Switch Will Make History'. Simple people who only wanted electricity and not history had their electric bulbs and gadgets ready. All 20 houses were suddenly lit up.

The oldest cottages here once held looms for the weaving of Kersey cloth, which is mentioned two or three times in Shakespeare, and nearby Lindsey produced what came to be known as Linsey Woolsey. Two hillsides form the village street with a stream crossing the road at the bottom. At the peak of one hill stands the church while upon the other are the ruins of a priory.

⌘ KESSINGLAND

How are the mighty fallen! Once, Kessingland could have taken on neighbouring Lowestoft with one hand tied behind its back and won. Now, everything indicates that it is merely a satellite of the flourishing seaside resort. The great number of houses and bungalows built in Kessingland since the war does nothing to change this opinion for these are largely people who sleep here but work elsewhere. Not that Kessingland is not itself flourishing in a changed and minor role chiefly concerned with the holiday trade.

But this is trifling compared to its importance in the Middle Ages. With a population then of about 8,000 mostly dependent on the port and herring fishing, it was busy enough to have a weekly market and an annual fair. At the time of the Norman Conquest, when Kessingland was required to pay a toll of 2,200 herrings from its sea-harvest, Lowestoft was not even mentioned. Then, as at Blythburgh, the fortunes of the port declined as the harbour silted up. Nevertheless, it has always provided some of the finest herring fishermen along the coast, some of them manning the boats at Lowestoft.

Brave men and strange men have lived here beside the sea. There was Edward Wigg, lifeboatman and head of generations of lifeboatmen, and Harry Smith, winner of the Stanhope Medal for the bravest deed of 1926 when he dived overboard in a storm and managed to save the life of a fellow crewman. There was Sea Row Jack, a man of means who chose to dress in skins and live in a wooden tower on the beach. In the close-knit community also lived Tidley, Bucko, Ike, Mouse, Yaller Iron, Spuff and Wonney among many other fishermen with nicknames.

⌘ KIRTON

There has been a considerable invasion of Suffolk villages by newcomers since the Second World War and Kirton is one of those surprised to find itself suddenly twice as big as it thought it was. It has an ideal position here just four miles from Felixstowe with its busy port yet managing to keep the look and feel of an old-time community. Past the tiny green one can walk right down to the Creek, an inlet of the Deben where once ferries crossed the river to Ramsholt and Sutton. Kirton Sluice it is called and it gives no hint now of its history, for, apart from the square, man-made little harbour, there is nothing left visible but the remains of an old barge. Once it was a sizeable port with many ships coming up the river and there is still a local belief that ships to face the Spanish Armada were built here.

The church of St Mary and St Martin lies pleasantly at the end of a side road from the village centre. It was mentioned in the Domesday Book but has nothing antiquated about it nowadays. The influence of new blood and new ideas can be seen at a glance. A beautiful porch welcomes the visitor into what could be the foyer of a first-class hotel but succeeds in blending perfectly with the main body of the church. Besides the new entrance, a great many improvements have been made and a church hall has been built nearby in which an astonishing number of village organisations are active.

A Brontë-type young woman lived here in the 18th century. She was Clara Reeve, a daughter of the rector and a determined writer who succeeded in getting her books published and indeed widely read by the standards of the time. A more recent character to inhabit the rectory was the Rev J. W. Weir, known far and wide as a man who answered only to his own conscience and who was indefatigable in his work for the less fortunate in our society.

At the White Horse inn they will tell you of what was once the great joke of the village. Kirton, it was said, was held together by rivets. Yes, by Rivetts. There were more Rivetts here than any other name, at one time with twelve large families. Truly enough, the village was held together with Rivetts.

⌘ LAVENHAM

Lavenham is probably the best-known village in Suffolk. Like Snape, it is the right sort of place to know. Like Kersey, it suffers a little from too many panegyrics of praise. I sometimes wish that visitors to these places would spare a little time to go also to the more typical villages around.

Lavenham is unique, of course, as an exhibition of medieval architecture. Where else could you find such a magnificent church in company with beautifully timbered houses? But there are no warts on this face of the Middle Ages, only well-preserved perfection. It is an idealised picture that arouses some indignation if anything exists to spoil it. An ardent admirer of Lavenham (in an analogy of Beauty and the Beast) writes: 'The church, of course, is the Beauty and wondrously beautiful it is but the thing that is incredible is that nobody has planted a row of trees or a glorious high hedge to hide the ugly rows of houses

A carved doorway in Lavenham

looking at the church.' Do people really want a town to be a museum? Perhaps some do. Others may reflect that wool towns were not all timbered mansions but had their hovels too, or the merchants would not have become rich.

Even more striking than the church, perhaps, is the wealth of memorable architecture round about. Here are the houses of the wool merchants, the Wool Hall and the incomparable Guildhall, with whole rows of medieval and Tudor houses of less importance. The basis of the prosperity that provided these buildings was originally the weaving of blue cloth and serge. Later, the trade continued in serge, shalloons, says, stuffs, calimancoes, hempen cloth and worsted yarn. There was also straw plaiting.

⌘ LAXFIELD

There is an invitation to pause in Laxfield's long and pleasantly wide village street, if only to gaze on the variety of dwellings, side by side as many are, but completely independent in style. The whole place retains an unmistakable atmosphere of old Suffolk. In this long street one can imagine a blacksmith and a wheelwright still plying their trade and a tumbril or two rumbling on their tall wheels towards the farms. I know that Laxfield likes to think of itself as progressive and so it is, but it also holds on to its past in a very positive way. Not many communities of this size have a museum and certainly not such a one as this, beautifully housed in the Guildhall beneath ancient beams.

The ancient Guildhall dates from 1461 and was first called the Cherchehous. Its religious connections aroused the disapproval of Henry VIII and it was given into the keeping of the lord of the manor.

The very impressive church is the work of different centuries but there was a church here in Saxon days and it was mentioned in the Domesday Book. The present fine 100 foot tower was erected in 1480 when a good deal of money accrued from local legacies.

Laxfield has a right to be proud of its past and of its present status but if there is anything of which it is slightly ashamed it must be that it gave house-room to the arch-vandal William Dowsing, who was born and bred here to become the lackey of the Commonwealth. He was appointed to rid the churches of 'superstitious' objects and pictures, which included the pictures in stained glass windows. No one could have carried out these orders more thoroughly. In 50 days he visited 150 churches and left a trail of havoc.

⌘ LETHERINGHAM

It is worth following the winding roads west of Wickham Market to find this pleasant but tiny village on the river Deben. Nearby are the ruins of a 14th century priory and church, both relics of a past age for the chancel of the church

Letheringham water mill stands beside the river Deben

has gone and the priory gateway that remains gives no more than a hint of its early importance as a cell of the Black Canons of Ipswich. It was Sir Robert Naunton, Secretary of State under James I, who ultimately took over the priory after the Dissolution and turned it into a mansion, complete with moat. The Naunton family lived here for several generations but eventually the estate devolved upon William Leman, who dismantled much of the old Hall.

There is a water mill still standing beside the Deben here and it makes a favourite beauty spot in the summer. On dark nights when the wind howls it would probably have less appeal for it is known that a number of skeletons were found in the miller's garden in 1844. The story is that murders were committed by an enraged ex-employee of the miller named Jonas Snell. At that time a Mr Bullard and his son were running the mill and were both killed but Snell was soon caught and was executed at Wickham Market six weeks later.

⌘ LIDGATE

When the ancient castle that stood on a mound here fell into disuse, its ruins were speedily used to repair medieval roads. In its place arose the handsome church of St Mary, that could not have been more than a century old when it gave sanctuary and hope to a nameless boy. He was to be John Lydgate, who took the name of the village for his own and made it resound throughout the land.

John was fortunate among his contemporaries. He was given his early education at the monastery of Bury St Edmunds and because of the promise that he showed was sent to Oxford. He was much influenced by the authors that he admired so much: Boccaccio, Dante and especially Chaucer who was about 30 years older than he. With literary leanings himself, Lydgate sometimes sent his poems to Chaucer for his approval.

Lydgate's literary energy was vast. For his patrons, who included both Henry V and Henry VI, he would turn out ballads, hymns and poems as required for masque, may game or mumming. Apart from this he was usually engaged in writing vast screeds of poetry. One poem, called the *Falls of Princes*, was nine times longer than Shakespeare's *Hamlet*. Perhaps they were read by a few people at a time when Chaucer had whetted their appetite for literature. But the promise of the 'monk of Bury' as he called himself was never fulfilled save in his tireless industry. One may look in vain for a single word of his in any dictionary of quotations.

⌘ LONG MELFORD

It is worth the mile-long walk through the street at Long Melford just to see at close quarters the endless variety of styles and colours in the houses, the pubs and the shops, all in close proximity in this, the largest of our villages. As a reward for the effort there is the great church of Holy Trinity standing before you, magnificent in an oasis of green sward and with the beauty and proportions of a cathedral.

Inside the church is an unusual marble font and an alabaster relief of the Adoration of the Magi. There is a small chapel called the Clopton Chantry which was intended for prayers to be offered up for the souls of the Clopton family of Kentwell Hall.

There are three great houses here all close by the village street. Melford Hall is a moated Tudor mansion with towers crowned with domes and with a garden that shows, with all else, the skill of the topiary artist. It was once the pleasure house of the abbot of Bury until such religious privileges were disposed of. Kentwell Hall is another Elizabethan house with moat and bridges, the home once of the Clopton family. Also looking onto the village street is Melford Place, home of the ancient family of Martyns. The Martyns, Cloptons and the Cordells are all remembered here in the church. Sir William Cordell, who built the fine almshouses on the

The gateway to the Tudor Melford Hall

green, who welcomed Queen Elizabeth to the town and who held high office under both the Tudor queens, lies in an elaborate tomb with a marble canopy and with the Virtues of Prudence, Justice, Temperance and Fortitude watching over him.

⌘ MELTON

Melton joins itself equably to the town of Woodbridge without any noticeable break and then carries on along a fine, straight road to the village proper. It is at Melton's river bridge that we are allowed the first crossing of the Deben from its estuary at Felixstowe. Over Wilford Bridge lie the scenic areas of the Heritage Coast, but there is enough open space here for the visitor to relax, have a quiet walk or a picnic among the bracken or on the edge of the forest areas.

The village of Melton keeps itself properly to its side of the bridge, nursing the beautiful church and the community centre which has been spared the trials of passing traffic by the introduction of a by-pass road. The elegant church spire looks down on a particularly handsome exterior and a churchyard with nary a tombstone in sight. Instead, the church is surrounded by smooth, well-cut lawns and rose beds. There is a memorial in one of the windows where the Victorian novelist Henry Seton Merriman is given the importance his books once earned by their wide popularity. Merriman lived here and was only 41 when he died.

A mile or so along the old road to Wickham Market is the entrance to St Audry's Hospital, once officially called the Suffolk Lunatic Asylum and in my young days simply the Melton Asylum. Unfortunately this was usually reduced further to 'Melton' so that a slight opprobrium attached itself to the place. St Audry's was originally a House of Industry but has recently been taken over by developers and the attractive grounds are filled with expensive homes in what is now called Melton Park.

⌘ MENDLESHAM

What was it that caused the creation of this very large and ancient village in the first place? There are two quite long and closely-packed streets of houses called Front Street and Old Market Street, now designated a conservation area, and several small off-shoots. Through the centuries the mainstay has undoubtedly been agriculture though some weaving was done and a regular market held at one time. There is a weaver's window in Front Street and a retting pit still

Mendlesham's ancient Front Street

Middleton

discernible in a nearby field where flax was soaked before it was worked.

Mendlesham has that odd characteristic seen in one or two other villages round about, of having a major community in one place and a kind of satellite village a couple of miles away. In this case the lesser hamlet is called Mendlesham Green.

Situated at the base of both village streets is the beautiful church built on the site of an earlier Saxon church. The 13th, 14th and 15th centuries all had a hand in the building. Among the remarkable objects to be found in the church is a font cover that reaches up in a great pyramid of magnificent style and decoration. It was made in 1630 by John Turner, a craftsman of Mendlesham. Another notable craftsman was Daniel Day, who in the 18th century had a workshop in Front Street where he produced the rare and latterly much-valued Mendlesham chairs. Two of the chairs can be seen beside the altar.

More exciting, and the object of many a visitor from far-off places, is the priest's chamber. Here, up some steep stairs and within the well-guarded room is a rare collection of medieval and Tudor armour. There are 23 pieces altogether, including an Elizabethan long-bow.

⌘ MIDDLETON

Here is an example of a Suffolk village which has completely disappeared. It was called Fordley and it stood beside Middleton on the heathland beside the little river Minsmere. Each village had a church but so close together they shared the same churchyard and a great deal of hostility grew up between the two parishes because of the sound of each other's church bells. If the times of the Sunday services were not synchronised, the congregation of one had to suffer interruption of their service by the noise of the other. The two clergymen in office shared the animosity of their separate parishes and would make no effort to stop the nuisance. In the end, a petition was sent by churchgoers to the Bishop of Norwich, who ordered that there should be one minister only and he should officiate at both churches alternately. In those days, when every church had its parson, the judgment was regarded as being akin to Solomon's.

The identity of little Fordley soon began to disappear. The two parishes merged as Middleton-cum-Fordley. Now all references to Fordley and all traces of its church have gone. On the other hand, Middleton became a substantial community, enjoying a score of craftsmen including five shoemakers.

A separate part of the village is called Middleton Moor, and though this is an unusual term in Suffolk, the appearance of the windswept expanse of grass here proves that it is not badly named. The proximity of heathland always provides a certain air of desolation and this is carried into the very centre of this small community.

⌘ MONK SOHAM

Just outside the village proper is Hungers Green. It could, of course, refer to someone's name but if it means what it seems to mean it is in good company. In different parts of the county I have come across Hunger Hall (twice), Hungergut Hall, Starknaked Farm and Threadbare Hall. I have looked in vain for Abundance Hall or Repletion Hall.

Monk Soham, as the name suggests, was the resort of monks before the Reformation and whether they came for penance or for pleasure there is no doubt there was a constant interchange with the abbey at Bury St Edmunds. Fishing they certainly indulged in for the fishponds they used can still be identified. But, as with all such establishments, the heyday came to an end and Henry VIII gave the manor to Antony Rous who sold it to Lionel Tolmach soon after Elizabeth's accession.

The church contains many early treasures, with a font as old as the chancel itself and a Jacobean chair and magnificent iron-bound chest. It also has a sprinkling of monuments to devoted servants. Rectors had notoriously long lives even in the days when so many of the population died young. Here lived the longest of all, the

Rev F. Capper, credited with 59 years in the pulpit. Beside him, the incumbency of Fitzgerald's great friend Robert Groome of 44 years, seems moderate.

⌘ NACTON

Here lived Broke of the *Shannon*, hero of the battle against the American frigate *Chesapeake* in 1813, and close by lived the wealthy Vernon family whose admiral was the one who captured Porto Bello. The wooded slopes of their estates stretched side by side down to the foreshore of the river Orwell.

Broke House had been built about 1767 though the family had lived there at what was called Cow Haugh since 1526 when Sir Richard Broke established the estate. Larger and more ostentatious was the home of the Vernons, the vast Orwell Park mansion that was built in the 18th century.

For all the extent of the Broke and Vernon estates and the keepers paid to protect them, smuggling used to take place all along the river. The exploits of one of these smugglers and the Nacton servant girl, Margaret Catchpole, unfortunate enough to fall in love with him form one of the best-known of Suffolk's stories.

The story tells of a spirited girl who was persuaded to steal a horse from her employer and ride it pell-mell to London to meet her lover Will Laud, how she escaped from prison to meet him yet again and saw him shot down by her side and how at last she was deported to Australia. There she became an unofficial nurse to the settlers' families, became deeply interested in the country's affairs and sent back to England many of the examples of wildlife that she discovered.

Margaret was a remarkable girl. Youngest but one in a family of six children. She taught herself to read and write and at the age of thirteen showed herself capable of quick thought and action. She had been sent to a neighbouring farm with a message and on arrival there found the mistress in a fit and the servants standing around helplessly. Margaret immediately gave instructions to the servants, ran out to the yard and discovered the only horse, a young Punch with only a halter around its neck. In an instant she was galloping into Ipswich to fetch a doctor, without saddle or bridle, her clothes and hair flying.

⌘ NAYLAND

This is another pearl in that beautiful necklace of villages that spreads itself along the north bank of the river Stour. It has been loved by many, including John Constable who painted the altar picture for the church of St James. The picture is one of only two religious works that Constable painted.

At the height of the Suffolk weaving industry, Nayland was one of the most prosperous cloth-making centres – only Lavenham and Boxford produced more. The evidence of solid affluence over the centuries can be seen in the substantial, individually-styled houses and in the impressive size and elegance of the church.

In 1552 there were 14 clothmakers, each one an employer of weavers, fullers and shearmen. One well-to-do clothmaker named William Abell left his mark literally in the fabric of the village. Having built the single-span arched bridge across the Stour to Essex, he turned his attention to the church and constructed its most handsome porch. In it he proudly added a simple logo of his name, a capital A within the shape of a bell.

The splendid church was built about 1400 on the site of an even older church. There is a memorial to that distinguished churchman, musician and scientist, the Rev William Jones, who became curate here in 1777. To his everlasting remorse, he was a distant member of the family of Oliver Cromwell, whom he despised. His brother-in-law had been one of the judges at the trial of Charles I and had suffered execution at the Restoration. In the eyes of the Rev Jones this did not absolve his family's part in the death of the king and he felt the shame so acutely that each year he set aside the anniversary of that day as one of penance.

⌘ NEEDHAM MARKET

Needham's water mill

Ups and downs occur in all village histories in varying degrees; in the case of Needham Market there seems to have been a preponderance of misfortunes. To begin with, it is not very flattering to know that Needham (without the suffix) is simply 'a hamlet of Barking' or that, at one time, the signs of decay and desolation in the village were such that the simile 'as poor as Needham' became a common saying.

It was not always so. In the Middle Ages the place was busy and prosperous, with a considerable trade in woollen goods and a weekly market on Wednesdays. Each year in October there was a fair for cattle and general merchandise. But catastrophe arrived in 1685 when a revival of the plague struck the community. It brought an end to the good times, the market was abandoned and the production of woollens gradually lost to newer processes elsewhere. It was a long time before the village could re-establish itself but local agriculture, milling and a paper factory sustained the population over the difficult years. In 1793 a determined effort was made to recover lost prosperity by dredging the river Gipping, allowing barges to come up the river from Ipswich to the mill and beyond to Stowmarket.

Needham Market teeters on the brink of being a town and the extensive building projects all around have certainly boosted the population considerably. The long main street is closely built with houses and shops of all kinds, buildings that are ancient and varied but of no great distinction. The little church stands beside the houses in the street and it has the finest hammerbeam roof in the country.

⌘ NEWBOURNE

Newbourne lies exactly in the centre of the triangle formed by the towns of Ipswich, Woodbridge and Felixstowe. It is one of the few villages that can claim a complete transformation, thanks to the Land Settlement Association and the government policy between the wars of giving aid to unemployed miners. Until the time that researchers decided that Newbourne was ideal for settlement, it was no more than a mere hamlet. The church overlooked a few cottages and the Fox Inn from its raised situation among the trees, and the old Hall nearby held nothing but its memories. The new 'settlement' changed it all.

It was a brave new scheme. Each 'settler' was provided with a 5-acre plot on which was a brand-new house, a range of piggeries and outbuildings and a large greenhouse. Assistance was given in the way of practical advice by experts and financial aid in the purchase of essential requirements like tools and fertilisers. There was also a well-planned organisation for collecting, transporting and marketing all produce from the holdings. It must have seemed a very strange environment to the families who had cut themselves off from their northern roots but most of them hung on through good times and bad and became part of the indigenous population – 'settlers' no more.

In the graveyard of the fine old 14th century church is the tombstone of the Suffolk Giant. George Page was said to be 7ft 7in tall. He travelled the country to be exhibited in sideshows, usually with his brother who was also of massive size. Little more is known of them though there have been fictionalised accounts of their lives.

⌘ ORFORD

The bonus for the traveller to Orford is that the whole journey from Melton onwards is through a beautiful countryside of forest and heath. With a score of roadside areas to stay and relax in, it is not a course to be rushed but rather to savour and smell the heather and the clean air from the sea. Then, quite contrary to Stevenson's dictum that it is better to travel hopefully than to arrive, the little town itself will welcome you with a charm all its own.

The castle is the great attraction, as it deserves to be, for this must be one of the finest and best-preserved keeps in the whole country. The 90 foot high fortified tower stands just beside the village centre on grassy undulations that still mark the ancient ditches and it looks out across the river to the marshes of Orford Ness.

The castle was threatened with demolition in 1805 by the Marquis of Hertford until it was pointed out by coastguards that it was a valuable landmark for shipping. By keeping the castle in line with the church ships were

Orford viewed from the river Ore

assured that they were following a proper course that would avoid the dangerous Whiting sand-bank.

Seaward of the castle, the terrain is much affected by the odd behaviour of the river Alde which initially flows toward the sea but changes its mind at the last moment and turns south to run parallel to it. The peninsula so caused is almost entirely of mud and marsh. It makes a fine sanctuary for certain kinds of birds including the avocet, a colony of which have commonly nested on the marshes of Havergate Island.

⌘ OTLEY

Otley spreads itself comfortably in good farming country close to the ancient estate of the Tollemaches at Helmingham. It has its own handsome Tudor hall with bricks in herring-bone pattern between the beams, a house that once belonged to the Gosnold family. John Gosnold was a country gentleman who showed an extraordinary personal loyalty to three successive sovereigns. No other man could ever have known more of the private lives of public monarchs and his knowledge all but cost him his head and certainly lost him his beloved home at Otley.

He was a gentleman-usher at the court of Queen Elizabeth I until her death, when he transferred his duties to the new king from Scotland, James I. Then, when Charles became king, Gosnold was appointed a gentleman of the Privy Chamber. Someone so close to the king could not hope to escape when the king was beheaded and punishment came in the shape of heavy fines, so harsh that the estate at Otley had to be sold.

⌘ OULTON

This is the gateway to the Broads, a place for summer leisure and holiday indolence, standing between Lake Lothing to the east and the expansive Broad to the west. Boating in one form or another is the entire, absorbing commitment of the village, its *raison d'être*. Those who are not actually afloat are doing something to boats or watching those who are doing something to boats. Not many, perhaps, will have time to stare at the ancient church beside the water or to stay to pay homage to that grandiose character Sir John Fastolfe who lies here. The old warrior had fought in France, enjoying the victory at Agincourt but suffering defeat at the hand of the Maid of Orleans had returned to be immortalised as Falstaff in the plays of Shakespeare.

But if Fastolfe will not tempt the would-be sailors from their boats, there is another literary association that may well do so. George Borrow spent the last years of his life here within sight of the Broad and in his summer-house under the trees wrote his most memorable works – *Lavengro, The Bible in Spain* and *The Romany Rye.*

Peasenhall, an 'old-timer' of a village

Borrow was born at East Dereham in Norfolk and he dutifully followed his father's wish that he should become a lawyer and was articled to a solicitor in Norwich. But when his father died, he found the door to freedom was wide open and took to the open road where for long periods his only companions were gypsies and fairground prize-fighters. He learned the gypsy language and their customs and when he came back to live at Oulton, it was of gypsies and the wonder of open-air freedom that he wrote. He seemed to capture the very essence of that world in the words spoken by the gypsy Petulengro: 'There's day and night, brother, both sweet things; sun, moon and stars, brother, all sweet things; there's likewise a wind on the heath. Life is sweet, brother.'

⌘ PEASENHALL

This is a real old-timer of a village, large enough to have a street that is long and continuous, though nicely higgledy-piggledy. It is a place that tells of crafts and skilled, busy men serving the needs of the rural hinterland. Why the community settled here and how it managed to survive must rest simply on local agriculture and the industry of craftsmen. Here in Peasenhall the farmers and their workers as well as the gentry could always obtain the basic goods and services that made life tolerable.

At about the time of Queen Victoria's accession the list of craftsmen was at its peak. Three blacksmiths, three shoemakers and three wheelwrights working, a saddler and collar maker, a cooper and a bricklayer, two carpenters and a plumber and glazier. In business there was a corn merchant and an enterprising family turning out seed and manure drills. Carriers plied regularly between Peasenhall and Norwich, Ipswich and Colchester. It was a hive of industry and not at all a likely setting for the murder that was to take place at the turn of the century.

This celebrated case concerned the murder of a young village servant girl, Rose Harsent. Suspicion settled upon William Gardiner, a business man and a pillar of the local Methodist church. At the trial, one juror prevented a unanimous verdict of guilty and a re-trial was ordered. Again the jury disagreed and Gardiner was acquitted. General belief, then and since, concludes that he was guilty but escaped justice by the bungling of the prosecution and the use of a very aggressive barrister on his behalf. Certainly Gardiner did not stay to test local opinion – he immediately shaved off his beard and left the village for good.

⌘ PIN MILL

There are sailors that must go down to the sea again and those who prefer to stay in the river. At Pin Mill there is an abundance of the latter kind, forming a considerable fleet of small leisure craft that threatens to overflow into the neighbouring marina at Woolverstone. Besides its small, modern boats, Pin Mill is also renowned for its tradition of barge sailing. The Pin Mill Barge Match is held each year on a Saturday in July when stout old vessels of long service would sail to the estuary and back. It was a silent, graceful and yet still supremely exciting competition and people lined the shores of the Orwell to watch.

The name of the village has aroused much speculation in the past. One school of thought believes that it owes its origin to a local *grande dame* named Elizabeth Woolverston. A list of her possessions on her death included two mills on the banks of the Orwell, given to her by her father as 'pin money'. A more erudite line is that the name comes from 'pynd' or 'pennd' which in early English described a mill pond of fresh water.

Many illustrious barges have sailed from here, none more worthy than the old *Tollesbury* that made the Little Ships journey to Dunkirk in 1940 and rescued nearly 400 tired soldiers from the beaches.

At the end of the war, when many countries felt that they owed a debt of gratitude to Britain, Swedish radio broadcast a programme on Suffolk and Pin Mill in particular, pointing out the individual sacrifices it had made for victory. It ended: 'The county of Suffolk was foremost in volunteer work in the war. It was

The busy hard at Pin Mill

first in England to get out a survey of its population resources and industry for post-war planned development ... The village of Pin Mill, which was steadfast in war, is also determined to be in the vanguard of progress in peace.'

⌘ PLAYFORD

The message that Playford gives out is that it is not just a pretty place, though that is true enough. Unlike many villages that keep themselves very much to themselves, Playford offers any visitor who has two feet and is willing to use them a chance to become better acquainted.

It has been my great delight for many years to take advantage of this opportunity. There are footpaths here through beautiful countryside in all directions. A favourite of mine is to follow the course of the Fynn to Aldercarr or alternatively to take the Warren Path past the woods to Donkey Lane. There is a maze of paths here, many of them beckoning towards the neighbouring village of Tuddenham. What could be better than to come out at last beside the Fountain Inn? If ever you tire of walking in that direction you can go by the quiet back road past the high-banked church that is mantled in trees and try the Squeech Path into Pigs Valley, where you will find no pigs but a plantation of rustling poplars. The wonder is that so few ever set foot in these delightful ways into the rural heartland. When the traffic is steaming and hissing on the main roads, here is a retreat, a solace that cannot be valued enough.

An obelisk in the churchyard pays tribute to an occupant of Playford Hall for thirty years whose modesty kept him almost unknown among the great reformers. Thomas Clarkson, a schoolmaster's son destined for the church, became an MA of Cambridge and in the course of his final examinations wrote a thesis on human slavery. His studies brought him to believe that this must be one of the most enormous sins of mankind, and he thenceforward devoted his entire life to the fight for abolition.

His energy was unremitting. Wherever in Britain there were merchants, ship owners or profiteers engaged in the trade, there he would carry his crusade. As his influence extended, he travelled to France and Russia to assist in their campaigns. He lived to hear of the Emancipation Act and he came back to Playford to spend the last years of his long life in this peaceful village.

⌘ POLSTEAD

The peaceful pool at Polstead

There are so many attractive aspects to Polstead – the pond or pool place – it seems a pity that most visitors come only because of a crime committed here in the 19th century. The Murder in the Red Barn has since been celebrated widely in story and melodrama. Even now, when violence becomes more frequent and more bizarre, the fascination of the story remains. The Red Barn was burned down long ago and the tombstone marking Maria Marten's grave has been despoiled and broken away to nothing. Only the cottage remains that housed the poor girl.

Polstead's beautiful church of St Mary was built around 1160, when Henry II was king and Archbishop Thomas à Becket had a precious few more years before his murder. There have been some alterations but the Norman characteristics are there for all to see. In the 14th century a tower was added and later still a spire was placed on top of the tower, the only surviving stone spire in the county.

In this attractive valley of the river Box the village of Polstead has added its own kind of beauty in the spring when acres of cherry trees have blossomed as a prelude to the crop of famous black cherries. Appreciative new villagers have raised the community awareness of the charms of the environment and work hard to keep all in good order. In the churchyard, stones have been levelled and rose bushes planted by bereaved relatives of the dead. It all looks very tidy and it helps the grass-cutting, they say.

Well, it is some sort of achievement. But I wonder if the time will come when we will search – as we already do for old objects, old places, old innocence – for an old-fashioned churchyard with its gravestones all awry and half-hidden in ox-eye daisies and buttercups. Tidiness is not all nor is practical expediency the final answer.

⌘ RATTLESDEN

Rattlesden is a place that asks to be visited simply for the old-world charm that still exists. It is a large and open village with several greens or commons and picturesque houses, a place where one can rest and forget the rest of the world. The only spectacular feature, which some older villagers deprecate as being unsuitable, is the pair of huge whalebones erected into a pointed arch near the bridge. Close observation of the changing condition of the bones has convinced at least one local man that it is possible to foretell the weather from them.

The village stands at one of the sources of the river Gipping and once received barges here that had sailed all the way from Ipswich. The Port of Bury St Edmunds, it has been called, though people would probably smile at the description nowadays. Stone for the cathedral was brought here by boat and in later centuries so was contraband. From this point goods legal and illegal were put onto carts and carried overland. Such activity at the riverside is difficult to imagine now, for the tributary of the Rat is not much more than a good-sized ditch. A few years ago a

The spaciousness of Rattlesden

great controversy grew up locally when it was suggested that the name Rat should be changed. Happily, it is still the Rat and the stalwarts who opposed the change can sleep peacefully until the next village crisis.

⌘ REDGRAVE

For much of the past, particularly in the 18th and 19th centuries, the village has been dominated by Redgrave Hall, whose estate was once something like 20,000 acres and no doubt the employer of most of the peasantry. The lordship of Redgrave was first given to the abbey of Bury by Ulfketel, Earl of the East Angles, who was killed in 1016 in a battle against the Danes. At the Dissolution of the Monasteries, Henry VIII gave the manor to Thomas Darcy from whom it passed to the Bacon family, whose power and influence is recorded in many village histories.

The Hall was built by Sampson, Abbot of Bury, in 1211, then later, under the ownership of the Bacon and then the Holt families, the Hall and its territory became of baronial proportions although, when Queen Elizabeth visited in 1577, she thought it rather small. In or about 1770, the lord of the manor at that time, Rowland Holt, rebuilt the house and spent a fortune on improving the immediate landscape. In the great park were gardens laid out by Capability Brown and an immense lake of 45 acres.

Rowland Holt also paid for substantial restructuring of the church, including a new tower built of Woolpit bricks. Among the rectors here was one Thomas Wolsey, instituted in 1506, an ambitious churchman who was to become a Cardinal.

The Redgrave of today makes a charming picture with its open green and roadside pond in the centre. It also possesses a natural phenomenon that must be unique. Nearby are the sources of both the Waveney and the Little Ouse, each arising from a spring and each going in the opposite direction to the other. On the map it looks the same river, the border between Suffolk and Norfolk, but here is the unexpected truth. The Waveney flows eastwards and the Little Ouse westwards and both have their origin here.

⌘ RICKINGHALL

Whether Inferior or Superior, it comes to much the same thing – a long straight

Rickinghall stands on an old coaching route

street which they share with Botesdale. Where each begins and ends is a matter for the local purist as there is no obvious dividing line. The street on which they all stand is the old coaching route between Norwich and Bury St Edmunds and somehow it seems a little bemused by the activity of the present day.

Rickinghall Inferior has a round Norman tower to its church which is on the site of an earlier Saxon building. Additions were made to the church in the 13th and 15th centuries with a porch and a priest's room above. The colourful east window remembers the daughter of a Victorian rector, a popular girl who went happily on her honeymoon to Switzerland in 1870. By a tragic accident she fell into a crevasse and her body was never recovered. The beautiful church of Rickinghall Superior dates from the 14th century. There is still a stone stairway to a room over the porch and a continuous stone seat on both sides of the nave.

The lordship of the Rickinghalls was given to the monks of Bury by the Earl of East Anglia, Ulfketel. Henry VIII granted it to Nicholas Bacon with other lordships in the area and it was then bought by the Holt family. Sir John Holt was Lord Chief Justice and in his long career achieved a reputation for wisdom and tolerance, much needed in the days of witch-hunting and religious cruelty.

⌘ RUSHMERE ST ANDREW

Once a respectable amount of open space separated the village from Ipswich; now, part of it is already absorbed into the general plan of the town. However, all is not lost, by any means. There is still a good slice of heathland belonging to the villagers and, away from the busy main roads, the village image is desperately maintained. The quiet road that runs by the church is perhaps a little self-consciously rural, with hedges and trees, an authentic pond and authentic ducks. But there are no authentic peasants sucking on straws.

The situation of the village, on the edge of a large town with an open expanse of common at its disposal, has not always been a boon. In these days the heath is given over chiefly to the golf course and the walking of dogs but local pastimes have not always been so innocent. Public hangings drew huge crowds in the 18th century and Rushmere had the space to entertain a concourse of spectators. The *Ipswich Journal* of 10th April 1790 has this paragraph: 'Three men have been executed at Rushmere in the presence of a great crowd of people. The men spoke soberly and all behaved in a penitent manner. The one named Mills addressed the crowd and exhorted them to take warning from their condition. Then they joined hands and were launched into eternity.'

⌘ SNAPE

It is an astonishing thing to come across this collection of maltings and reflect that this is a place famed for music perhaps the world over. Music, opera, virtuosi in the

Snape Maltings concert hall and the river Alde

midst of these familiar sugar-beet fields? Who could have imagined such a thing? The buildings, the village and the river look much as they did when I used to watch the men shovelling the barley on the maltings floor.

There is another name beside those of artists and musicians which is important in the history of the place – Garrett of Leiston. At the Garrett engineering works, two brothers took over the business started by their father. Later, they separated, Richard the elder remaining in charge of the works while Newson took over the maltings at Snape, gradually extending the buildings there until they covered seven acres.

At the height of the Garrett business the Alde was a busy highway. There were twelve ships plying for Newson and as many bringing in iron ore for Richard. Newson Garrett died at the age of 82, leaving behind a large family; most famous of them was his favourite daughter Elizabeth, who, as Elizabeth Garrett Anderson, became the country's first woman doctor and the first woman mayor.

In the 1960s local maltings were being closed all over the country. At Snape the wooden shovels were put away forever in 1965. By chance the Aldeburgh Festival Committee was then looking for a permanent home and the brilliant idea of using the maltings was mooted. Benjamin Britten, the inspiration of the festival, had lived in a windmill at Snape and so the choice was appropriate. The story of the courage and enterprise in transforming the old maltings is well known. The triumph was shared by many who knew or cared little for music but who admired the determination of those who were so dedicated.

⌘ SOMERLEYTON

Like the whimsical river Alde further south, the Waveney shows a wilful nature when it approaches the sea. Almost within sight of it at Lowestoft, it then turns pettishly north-west and after losing itself in Breydon Water comes out finally at Yarmouth. It creates what is virtually an island here in the north-east corner of the county, in the centre of which is the village of Somerleyton.

The reputation of lordly splendour here comes chiefly from the famous Hall, now largely Victorian but still gracious and magnificent. It is set in the beautiful park of which Fuller once said – 'Sommerley Park is well named for here Summer is to be seen in the depth of winter in the pleasant walks on both sides, with fir trees green all the year long'.

It was Sir Samuel Morton Peto, made wealthy by the railway boom, who made spectacular changes to the village during his occupation of the Hall. Apparently a man of great energy and spirit, he constructed what came to be known as a model village around the green with a natural style of building that blended well with the rural scene. He then practically rebuilt the Hall and restored the church.

This may be Suffolk's forgotten corner so far as many are concerned but crowds of people make their way here in the summer months to view the grandness of the Hall, the spaciousness of the park and the magnificence of the trees. Not far away is the very popular stretch of water known as Fritton Lake and believed to be the most beautiful lake in East Anglia, lined as it is with woods and gardens.

⌘ THE SOUTH ELMHAMS

The mother-hen of South Elmhams sits on a clutch of six small villages in a very big backyard. Within the triangle of the towns of Harleston, Bungay and Halesworth a vast portion of the countryside is covered by the South Elmhams, whose total area must be counted in square miles. There are six separate communities, each named after a saint: All Saints and St Nicholas, St Cross or St George, St James, St Margaret, St Michael and St Peter.

The whole area of the South Elmhams is completely agricultural and deeply

The green at Somerleyton

rural. There is an atmosphere of past times in these villages that fits well with the sparse habitation.

The largest of the South Elmhams is All Saints and St Nicholas. Once they were separate parishes but the church of St Nicholas fell into ruins and was never rebuilt.

St Cross is large in area but very short of houses, with a small church which was repaired and re-pewed in 1841 to provide more sittings. Nearby a few ruins are left of an earlier church built in the 7th century.

St James is another straggling village that includes an area of arable land named St James' Park. This was once the site of the palace and demesne of the bishops of Norwich.

St Margaret is now a smaller village, with hardly enough local inhabitants to keep the place warm.

St Michael is even less populous – but it apparently holds on to what few it has. Eleven men went to serve in minesweepers in the war and all came back. Very few villages have this record.

At St Peter there is an ancient hall, now a farmhouse, which was the home of the wealthy Tasburgh family in days gone by.

⌘ STANTON

Going into Stanton from the direction of Ixworth, I had the opportunity for a few words with one or two people fortunate enough to live in this very pleasant community. The first man I spoke to was a stranger, I suspected, missing the signs of the dedicated countryman. He had been here for eighteen years, he told me. Well, as I thought, a complete stranger. A more aged gentleman treated me to some reminiscences in slow, familiar Suffolk speech. 'I'm glad you still use the dialect,' I told him. He looked blank. 'What dialect?' he said.

A handful of Stanton building workers were repairing a barn here around 1887, and, perhaps feeling that the Queen's Golden Jubilee required some special mark in history, wrote a patriotic message and placed it in a bottle which was hidden under the barn floor. The message, which was unearthed in 1948, said:

> 'This barn was repaired by Sturgeon Brothers but 65 years ago it was used as a Weslen Chapel: the part ware the bottle will be found was the door ware they went in.
>
> Theair will be grate rejoicing in England this year as it is the Jubilee year of Hear Majesty reign Queen Victoria. H. S. Dudding is the rector of this parish but the parish is to poor to do enney thing for the Jubilee but they are trying to get an organ for the church which will cost £120.'

Several names are added at the conclusion of the message together with the words – 'God Save the Queen'.

Once there were two separate parishes here of All Saints and St John, but the latter church long ago fell into ruins and the village is consolidated into one. The manor was given to the abbey at Bury by Edward the Confessor and granted after the Dissolution of the Monasteries to Sir Thomas Jermyn. The village had the right of a fair on Whit Monday and May 12th for the purpose of 'pleasure and pedlery'.

⌘ STOKE-BY-NAYLAND

About six miles from Hadleigh and just north of Nayland itself is one of our most illustrious villages. The church alone proclaims the fact to anyone who doubts it. The commanding tower with its triumphant corner pinnacles rises 120 feet into the sky and can be seen in all its glory from far and wide. It looks down on a nave and chancel of Tudor splendour. About the church is a cluster of fine timbered houses.

There are two mansions hereabouts with histories of distinguished occupants. Gifford's Hall came to the Mannock family in the reign of Henry IV and a long succession of Mannocks have followed. Within the church are many memorials to the family and in recent years even more Mannocks have been literally unearthed. During repairs in the parish church, a burial vault was found under the floor containing seven coffins.

Tendring Hall was once occupied by William de Tendring who had a grant of a

The church at Stoke-by-Nayland

fair and market here from Edward I. It later came into the possession of the Rowleys, first of whom was Admiral Sir William Rowley, Knight of the Bath.

Common folk have also prospered here in the past and best remembered of these is the draper who became Sir William Capel and Lord Mayor of London but was never quite able to resist flamboyant gestures where money was concerned. Having lent the king, Henry VII, a great deal of money, he was so overcome with the honour of feasting with his royal debtor that he threw the bonds on the fire.

⌘ STONHAM ASPALL

This is Stonham Aspall because it has to be differentiated from other Stonhams nearby. The name Aspall or Haspele belonged to the one-time lords of the manor here. The other Stonhams also have additions to the name. One is Stonham Earl, usually called Earl Stonham nowadays, because the lordship was once held by the Earl of Norfolk and afterwards by the Earl of Suffolk. The other Stonham accepts the designation Parva.

The village nestles among trees not far from the Norwich to Ipswich road and the vital institutions of church, school and public house are assembled close together at the end of the main street. The church is modestly beautiful in a leafy setting in which stands an unusual alabaster monument to a member of the Wingfield family that for a long time occupied Broughton Hall nearby.

Proud of its range of ten bells and a record of expert campanology, the church must have made its presence heard if not felt in the village. It is not surprising that the public house has joined the cause and calls itself 'The Ten Bells'.

⌘ STOWLANGTOFT

An unassuming village with a long name, a mile or so south of Ixworth. Langtoft is added because it was the name of the lords of the manor here and Stow on its own, though much easier to say, could be with a little effort confused with Stowmarket.

Long after the Langtofts held the manor came the eminent family of d'Ewes. A wall monument in the church shows Paul d'Ewes kneeling, with his two wives and eight children. Little did he know that one of this brood of infants would become a famous antiquarian and scholar. This was Simon (sometimes given as Symond) who was made a baronet in 1641 and impressed everyone with a promise to re-write the history of England but seldom got beyond the title page. He spent years studying documents and records of the Tower of London and would have been happy to do no more than this but through loyalty to the Puritan cause served as a member of the Long Parliament until, rather to his relief, he was expelled with 40 others by Colonel Pride.

The church is believed to have been built on the site of a Roman camp by Robert Dacy of Ashfield. Roman remains have been found in the vicinity including a pot full of coins and, not far off, a fine tesselated pavement. Before he died, the philanthropist and churchman Robert Dacy changed his name to that of his native village – Robert Ashfield.

⌘ STUTTON

Not many decades ago the villagers of Stutton were viewing the future of the community with considerable misgiving. There were too few young people, too few houses, too few jobs. It all seemed to point to a slowly decaying life-style, with loss of amenities and possibly the closing of the school. Since then, happily, there has been a complete rejuvenation. New blood and new energy has brought hope and enthusiasm. Newcomers and old have joined in the resuscitation and a community council formed to direct ideas and projects.

The village has had its ups and downs. As far back as the plague, so the story goes, misfortune was near at hand. At that time the village was clustered about the church which is now some distance away from the centre. The legend tells that the old village was burnt down to stop the spread of the plague and that the victims were buried in that slightly ghostly avenue to the church called the Drift.

There was a time when barges could come up the Stour and call at the wharf at Stutton Point to take on sugar beet and other agricultural produce. Although this is no longer possible, there is water enough nearby with the huge Alton reservoir filling a whole valley with the water needs of Ipswich and district. A near-casualty of the reservoir was the one remaining water mill of the two formerly here. Its fate was widely discussed and finally solved by dismantling the mill and setting it up again as a fascinating museum piece in the Rural Life collection at Stowmarket.

There must have been a sigh of relief from churchgoers when a proper organ was installed in 1902. From 1832 for several years music had been supplied by a barrel organ which played only 12 tunes. A great leap forward was made in 1849 when a second barrel organ with another 12 tunes was added. Ten more years passed with the bulk of the tunes in the hymnal barely used and there was jubilation when a harmonium was installed in 1850.

⌘ SUTTON

In my childhood, Sutton was a foreign land. We would look across the river Deben from the shore at Woodbridge and marvel at the woods and sloping fields on the other side. On special days we would be rowed across in the ferry boat to picnic there where savages were likely to attack and where pirates' treasure lay buried under every tree. Childish imagination is strong but it could not for a moment envisage the vast treasure that was later to be found in these fields.

Generally, of course, Sutton is reached by road over the bridge at Melton. Here

The entrance to the museum at Sutton Hoo

are large, flat fields and the village looks lonely in the open landscape which is nevertheless well fringed with trees as windbreaks. There are footpaths two or three miles long from the road to the river. One footpath leads the walker over private land to the area of Sutton Hoo, the site of the discovery of the famous burial ship.

Here, in the summer of 1939, was revealed the greatest archaeological treasure of England's history. One of a group of mounds was found to hold the remains of a Saxon burial ship. It was 82 feet long and was probably a rowing galley, built of wooden planks held by iron nails. Time had disposed of the wood but the nails and the impressions left by the timbers were clear to see. Most of the treasure lay on the floor in the centre of the ship, covered by rotted wood and sand. There were gold ornaments and buckles, a huge silver salver, a sword with a jewelled pommel and other priceless objects.

Detailed study of the ship and the treasure led to the belief that, though it had all the signs of a Viking funeral, this was a Saxon burial and probably that of Raedwald, King of the East Angles, who died about AD 625.

The National Trust has taken over the site's presentation. Their innovations include a superb museum with a replica of the burial chamber and a display of some of the actual treasures found.

⌘ TATTINGSTONE

Squire White certainly left his mark on the village. Either from a sense of humour or for some reason of his own he created what is known as the Tattingstone Wonder. It has stood there since 1742 when Mr White died and must have deceived a multitude of people in that time. It is a church – at least, to all appearances it is a church since it has a tower, ecclesiastical-looking windows and what seems to be nave and chancel. Closer attention shows that it is nothing of the kind, the tower has only three sides, there is a chimney or two and other signs of domestic rather than religious use. In fact, this reverential guise cloaks one or two cottages originally designed for Mr White's employees. No doubt it all gave the squire a chuckle or two. 'People are often wondering at nothing,' he is supposed to have said, 'I'll give them something to wonder at.'

An unmistakable village institution is St Mary's Hospital, which has climbed out of the early opprobrium attached to it as a Victorian workhouse and does its important work in an enlightened atmosphere. An inmate of the old workhouse for something like 20 years was Mrs Ann Candler, a woman who found release and hope in the writing of poetry. As a young bride she had been suddenly left destitute by her husband's desertion and had suffered considerable hardship before coming to St Mary's. Fortunately, her poems came to the notice of Mrs Elizabeth Cobbold, whose kindness and understanding was already known to others. Mrs Cobbold became Ann's patroness and arranged for publication of her poems. With a sum of money so raised, Ann Candler was able to leave the workhouse for private lodgings at Holton near Stratford St Mary, where she died in 1814 aged 74.

⌘ THEBERTON

It is strange to think that this quiet, almost forgotten village is inevitably associated with war and with warriors for there is nothing but kindness to be found here among the inhabitants. Even the churchyard bids the visitor welcome with the 'sitting stone' of old John Fenn, once rector of this parish. It is an altar tomb but invites the passer-by to sit on it. The church is old, with a Norman doorway and an odd, undersized octagonal tower.

It was in June 1917 when war came violently to the village. An enemy airship came silently from the skies over the sea, faltering and drifting after attacks by British planes. It crashed eventually here at Theberton and in the churchyard now, within a special enclosure, are the 16 graves of the German dead. For a time they were 'unknown' but in later years names were found.

Near the village's memorial to its dead once stood a machine-gun in memory of that great soldier, Lieut Col Charles Hotham Montagu Doughty-Wylie, VC, hero of many foreign campaigns before losing his life at Gallipoli. Col Doughty-Wylie

Near Theberton

had already fought with Kitchener in the Sudan and was wounded in the Boer War and again in some uprising in Turkey where his bravery saved many lives. In the bitter, tragic campaign of Gallipoli, Col Doughty-Wylie led a night attack to try to capture a fort. The attack was successful but at the very moment that his troops were cheering, their leader was struck by a bullet and killed.

The family of Doughtys lived at the Hall, built at the end of the 18th century by George Doughty, a High Sheriff of Suffolk. It was enlarged in 1850 and allows a fine view of the sea three miles away.

⌘ THORPENESS

Here was an ugly duckling of a village that was miraculously changed into a swan. A hundred or so years ago, Thorpe was an unconsidered hamlet of Aldringham, a community given over almost entirely to fishing. About 25 owners of local smacks governed the lives and the well-being of the total population.

The metamorphosis took place when the new century began and an imaginative planner named Stuart Ogilvy called in designers W. G. Wilson and F. Forbes Glennie to help him create a complete new holiday village. A landmark in the

Thorpeness Mere is perfect for boating

operation was the excavation of the famous Mere and at about the same time Thorpe took on another syllable to become Thorpeness.

The village itself consists of fairly modest-looking weather-boarded houses that fit in with the fishing tradition. Of much more interest to summer visitors is the Mere, about two miles along the coast road from Aldeburgh and an ideal boating lake for children. More surprising still is the edifice that has come to be known as 'The House in the Clouds'. Seeing it for the first time causes people to rub their eyes in disbelief. A house resting on the top of a square tower perhaps 80 feet high really looks like a 'House in the Clouds'. In fact, the 'house' at the top is a camouflaged water tank but the stem of the tower actually is a house and occupied by a family.

⌘ THE TRIMLEYS

The Trimleys, with Walton also, form an almost continuous chain of houses along the three miles of what was once the only road in and out of Felixstowe. A new road, complete with roundabout and flyover at Trimley St Martin, now takes the port traffic on to the faster system which goes over the impressive Orwell Bridge and beyond without entering Ipswich.

Both Trimleys are extensive in area, reaching over a mile to the shoreline of the Orwell in one direction and almost within sight of the Deben in the other. At the

Orwell foreshore, local inhabitants concerned about wildlife and footpaths, watch the expanding port of Felixstowe with alarm.

Perhaps the most interesting feature here is the situation of the two churches, St Mary's and St Martin's, built close beside the road and separated by only a few yards of land which forms the boundary of the two parishes. Persistent legend has it that the churches were built separately by two quarrelling sisters but local historians throw cold water on the idea. On the other hand, there seems to be no alternative explanation for the two churches to be rubbing shoulders in the same churchyard, so the theory of the warring sisters makes as good a story as any.

Nowadays the two are united as one parish, though in other respects they maintain separate identities. The Civil War produced some degree of havoc, with the interiors of both churches desecrated and both rectors expelled for expressing sentiments contrary to the cause of Puritanism.

St Martin's, somewhat deeper into agricultural land than St Mary's, once had three windmills in service. Two of them were rather close together and the local joke is that one of these was demolished because the miller considered there was not enough wind for both.

At the corner of St Martin's Green is displayed the very handsome village sign in the form of a portrait of Thomas Cavendish, Elizabethan sea-dog and local hero. Beneath the picture are the words attributed to him when far away from his native haunts:

> 'My God, said Thomas Cavendish, whatever may be-fall,
> I'll ever love dear Trimley and the oaks at Grimston Hall.'

The Cavendish family had been lords of the manor at Grimston Hall nearby for over 300 years when young Thomas began to show his zest for adventure and the sea. No doubt he had heard and admired the stories of Francis Drake's perilous voyages and in due course Cavendish imitated his hero in many respects. Like Drake he had many encounters with the Spaniards and survived many a hard battle. With Sir Richard Grenville, he accompanied Raleigh across the sea to his new colony in America and soon after had the opportunity to do what he most wanted to do – to follow Drake's example and to become the second Englishman to sail round the world. In 1586 he fitted out three ships and sailed westwards, returning home triumphantly two years later to be received as a national hero.

Cavendish set off again in 1591 with five ships on a voyage that seemed to court disaster from start to finish. Only 15 of the 76 crewmen ever returned and Cavendish himself became separated from his little fleet to die alone in some foreign clime.

⌘ TUDDENHAM ST MARTIN

The wandering river Fynn crosses under the road bridge here at the lowest point of

Tuddenham St Martin seen from across the fields

the village street. It is a pleasant walk to follow the river for a mile or so on either side of the road. The village is compactly housed with a variety of dwellings on both sides of the hill and all lies within the gentle ambience of the church of St Martin. The church lends an ageless dignity to the street, standing on high ground as it does and with its 15th century west tower crowned with battlements. In the north wall is a well-preserved Norman doorway and inside is a font that is almost as old.

It has been reckoned that the font may be the most ancient in the county. It has an octagonal bowl with carvings of a variety of creatures and an elegant tall cover. Modern craftsmen too have added their skill to the beautification of the church. A fine new chancel screen of oak taken from the windmills of Earl Soham and Ashfield was installed and dedicated at the end of the Second World War.

The east window tells a tragic tale of a young son of a rector, Alexander Paton, who lost his life soon after going to sea as a midshipman. On climbing a mast to secure a sail in a hurricane he was wrenched from his hold by the wind and lost in the sea. Another memorial is to Michael Wolversten, who fought gallantly for his king in the Civil Wars only to witness the monarch's execution. For his support of the Royalist cause, Wolversten lost his estates and almost his life by the brutal decrees of Cromwell.

⌘ TUNSTALL

It was once Tunstall-with-Dunningworth, a hamlet that is now completely lost save for Dunningworth Hall, but which once had its own church and rectory. There is a record of the church standing in 1520.

The church of Tunstall is a beautiful 14th century edifice embowered in trees, with many treasures surviving the gloating excesses of William Dowsing who – 'brake down 60 Superstitious Pictures' (probably in coloured glass) 'and broke in pieces the Rails; and gave orders to pull down the Steps'.

I suppose it would be possible for any village to make a rough graph of its changing fortunes in the last hundred years simply by using the figures of the school roll. At Tunstall they are certainly revealing:

(At opening)	1873	37 pupils
	1887	75 – but attendance erratic.
	1904	143
	1928	84
	1973	36

The school is now closed.

The first and last figures of a hundred years show almost exactly the same number of pupils. But at the beginning of the 20th century the school was bursting its sides, having doubled the roll in 17 years. How can one account for the rapid decline in the early twenties? Perhaps a combination of Great War losses, smaller families and the general drift from the land can explain it, for there was at that time no great use of farm machinery to reduce the number of workers.

For many years soil experiments were carried on here, mainly to investigate the effects of the use of lime and chalk on light lands, a project that was eventually taken over by the firm of Fisons.

⌘ UFFORD

This is another village with two communities. They were once called Upper Street and Lower Street and were about half a mile apart. Now, the term Lower Ufford applies to the part which is in fact the more important. This is the old village, with 15th century houses and an even earlier church huddling together close to the street and quaint enough to attract many visitors on summer days. Nearby is the road bridge over the narrowing river Deben, probably the original ford of Uffa.

Uffa was a Scandinavian invader who settled here in the 5th century. He was important, perhaps a king, because the Venerable Bede talks of Uffa and of Raedwald, King of the East Angles, in the same breath.

Ufford's ancient church, which shows herring-bone courses of ironstone from the local crag as well as sections of Caen stone, is generally believed to belong to the 12th century. Inside, its greatest treasure is the great font cover, surely the most elaborate in Suffolk and perhaps in the whole country. It is 18 feet high and is a decorative cone of exquisite workmanship.

The bridge over the river is where Uffa's ford once was

The High Street is now spared the thunder of traffic that for years took this route past the Crown Inn and the roadside houses. Now, the Crown has regained some of the peaceful charm more in keeping with its age. It was mentioned as long ago as 1524 and even today retains some of the features of its early days including a cheery and friendly atmosphere in the bars.

⌘ WALBERSWICK

That agricultural Suffolk would become a haven for artists and craftsmen would have seemed very unlikely years ago. Now, it is home for actors and writers, potters and painters, all with an avowed interest in the county. The whiff of the sea in old fishing villages has been one strong call to artistic instincts and it is not difficult to understand the popularity of such places as Walberswick.

Walberswick was once a fishing and shipping centre of some importance. In 1450 there were 13 barks trading with Iceland and the Faroe Islands while as many as 22 fishing boats were setting off from and landing on these beaches.

When the first small, thatched church was demolished in 1473, a magnificent new one was built with two aisles and two altars. It was fitting that such a prosperous village should have a church of majestic size, in particular to receive the prayers for those at sea. Then, as the fishing declined, so did the church's congregation. In 1585 the great bell of 1,700 pounds in weight was sold and a hundred years later a new and more modest church was fashioned out of the old.

In 1590 the manor came into the possession of Sir Robert Broke, who promptly took away the common land belonging to the villagers. Amid great bitterness the land was regained some years later but the power struggle continued with cattle being driven off the common by the squire's employees. In the end it came to a brutal, stand-up fight between the squire's henchmen and the local commoners exasperated to the limit. In the battle four men were killed. The place where the fight took place was afterwards named Bloody Marsh.

⌘ WALPOLE

The road south-west from Halesworth travels through some good farming land to find the modest village of Walpole. A Norman doorway guards the church and within there is a beautiful Jacobean altar-table but for once it is a chapel rather than a church that claims attention. This Congregational chapel is believed to be the oldest but one in the whole country, having been established in 1646 after having already served for 40 years as a meeting-house.

The old building is well-preserved, both inside and out, and seems to have been

Charming cottages in Walpole

constructed around the main support of a stout mast brought from a ship at Yarmouth. The mast and the galleries around give a brief impression of being in an old-time sailing vessel but this is soon superseded by a feeling of awe that this simple chapel knew village life in the time of Cromwell and all through the years since.

Walpole has reason to remember one of its sons. George Carver came from a poor family in the village and found it expedient to leave home early to seek his fortune. In a shrewd and energetic lifetime he came, indeed, to be a wealthy man. When he retired, he came back to Walpole to spend his fortune on supplying some of the needs whose absence in his own boyhood he could remember so well. Among his gifts are the almshouses for widows that would remedy for many women the hardship that his own mother knew.

⌘ WALSHAM-LE-WILLOWS

Walsham-le-Willows lies in the very centre of the square formed by Diss, Thetford, Bury St Edmunds and Stowmarket. It has many picturesque houses, some thatched and timbered, an ancient inn and a very noble-looking church. The tower of St Mary's is particularly striking with its chequered pattern of flints surmounted by proud battlements and high pinnacles. The spacious interior of the church was cleaned and beautified in 1843, when some ancient wall paintings were discovered

Walsham-le-Willows has many picturesque houses

under the many coats of whitewash. There is also a stone plaque that was once of romantic interest to village maidens who would hang garlands upon it.

No doubt the church was well-attended in 1767 when smallpox threatened. Surprisingly, the medical resources of the time seemed to feel that they were more than equal to the occasion, a point of view partly explained by the vast profits which could be made. Notices were displayed advising everyone to be inoculated or suffer dire consequences. Two surgeons and an apothecary were standing by to provide the service. 'Ladies and Gentlemen' could receive attention in private cubicles for a fee of 5 guineas each. 'Servants and Others' were attended to with less ceremony for $2^1/_2$ to 4 guineas.

⌘ WESTLETON

Here is a fine, spacious green in a triangle that slopes upwards to its apex. A few houses jostle along the sides and at the base is the White Horse Inn and a shady mere on which the ducks paddle. Like so many villages along the coast it has a

The shady mere at Westleton

slightly desolate air as if remembering, even in summer, the harsh winds from the sea.

Some of the houses, modernised and improved through they now are, were the homes of humble fishermen for there was little but fishing and farm-work to sustain life in days gone by. Once, nearly every cottage had a small brick kiln in the garden in which herrings were cured over smoking oak chips and for a time much store was placed on this cottage industry.

Westleton is one of our largest villages but is unusual in having no great mansion or hall of the kind that used to dominate most rural communities. Independence must have cost the locals dear since there were no hand-outs from the gentry and none of those benevolences and bequests that played quite an important part in well-endowed villages.

In the Middle Ages the village was prosperous since it was an important stage on the road to the flourishing port of Dunwich. Later it became the responsibility of the village to maintain its own piece of turnpike. Two toll houses were built and the right was granted to charge all travellers (except the Royal Family who conceivably could well have afforded it) for the privilege of passing over that stretch of road. The passage of animals, too, required duties and some frantic counting must have gone on sometimes at the fixed rate of 5d a score.

⌘ WICKHAM MARKET

Rackham's Mill at Wickham Market

There is no mistaking the centre of Wickham Market. The entire activity of the place devolves upon the little square where shoppers' cars are ever chock-a-block in the square. The shops look on with some relief now that the by-pass has siphoned off some of the heavy traffic from the narrow roads. Nearby is the handsome church, renowned for its tell-tale spire that forms a landmark – and a sea-mark too, I understand – for the uncertain traveller.

A market here was originally granted by Henry VI in 1440. In recent times it moved to nearby Campsea Ashe, which was a reasonable move since the railway station in that village is called Hickham Market.

There was once a Shire Hall here, a superior edifice in which was held the Quarter Sessions. When the Sessions were moved to Woodbridge, the lord of the manor of the time decided that the Shire Hall had no further use and proceeded to demolish it. The building materials were taken for the building of a farmhouse in Letheringham.

Perhaps the most notable character of Wickham Market's past was John Kirby, whose *Suffolk Traveller*, based on his exhaustive surveys of the county from 1732 to 1734, forms such a valuable reference to village life in those days.

⌘ WINGFIELD

The expanding power of the de la Pole family found a perfect setting for their ambitions here at Wingfield. Already they had made fortunes as merchants despite humble beginnings in the north and in 1331 William de la Pole became the first mayor of the city of Hull. When the de la Poles moved south to Suffolk, the manor and fortunes of the long-established Wingfield family were in the keeping of the heiress, Katherine Wingfield. At the marriage of Katherine to Michael de la Pole, the great name of Wingfield was lost to the village. They had been here since the days of the Conqueror and at one time boasted eight knights in the family, two of them with Orders of the Garter.

Soon the de la Poles became Dukes and Earls of Suffolk and Michael obtained a licence from the king to convert the manor house into a castle. It looks grand enough still in this quiet corner of the village beside the great common, with a moat and a causeway to the front entrance. On certain days of the year it is open to the public.

Church, college and inn rub shoulders at the top end of the village. The 14th century church is framed in trees and carries many memorials to the powerful families who have lived here, among them William de la Pole, first Duke of Suffolk and friend of the king, who led the English armies triumphantly in the French wars until defeated by the Maid of Orleans. Blamed afterwards for some of the ills of the nation at that time, he was impeached and banished but was brutally murdered by his enemies on the voyage.

The college stands beside the church. It was first erected about the year 1362 by the Wingfields for a master and nine priests. Nearby, in keeping with the sense of early feudal power in these parts, the inn is still called the De La Pole Arms.

⌘ WITNESHAM

Witnesham straggles for two or three miles along the road between Ipswich and Debenham. There are two long and (for Suffolk) quite steep hills with some consolidation of housing in each valley. In one of these valleys, the Barley Mow is well-known in these parts and sometimes in other parts too as it occasionally featured in the cartoons of Giles, who lived nearby.

The other valley, called the Burwash, has another group of houses and a lane that leads off to the church. Close to the border with Swilland, the former Area School spreads itself across the head of a meadow. The Area School was not the first in the village. In 1840 there was a voluntary National School, largely financed and run by a kindly rector. It was at the beginning of the centralisation in rural districts in the 1930s that Area Schools were deployed in chosen situations to take the children from several villages. In the 1940s and 1950s, children arrived from about seven villages round about, on foot or on 'Committee' bicycles. (The Education Committee later became the Local Education Authority.)

At this north end of the village is also the moated mansion of Berghersh House, for long years the home of the Berghersh family after Sir Bartholomew Berghersh arrived in the reign of Edward III. By chance, the same king saw the first arrivals of the Meadows family, seated here ever since that time. At Witnesham Hall, just beyond the church and close by the spot where the Fynn begins its meandering course to the Deben, was born the famous naturalist, William Kirby. Kirby was no great explorer but saw the wonder of the nature that was close at hand, removing himself only to the neighbouring village of Barham where he stayed as rector for the whole of his long life.

⌘ WOOLPIT

The distant past from which legends arise provides Woolpit with stranger stories than most villages can claim. There were wolf-pits here, we are told, as long as a thousand years ago that were intended for the destruction of wolves. Then we hear that, centuries later, small green children emerged from the wolf-pits but we are inclined to view this phenomenon with justifiable doubt. Then there was the spring called Lady's Well in a meadow by the church, once believed to be of great curative powers, particularly for sore eyes; tradition tells of many pilgrims who came to a chapel beside the spring.

Wolves, green children and perhaps even people with sore eyes are notably absent from modern Woolpit which, like many other villages in recent years, has been by-passed by a new road system and left in comparative peace. It is never

Woolpit's village pump, now grandly roofed

like the golden days of yore, of course; traffic is reduced but not banished. Nevertheless, there is time and space enough to admire the many kinds of homes here, from the straightforward modern to the picturesque, timbered Weaver House. Flint and brick, timber and thatch cohabit here in complete harmony. Some of the buildings, including the Swan Inn and the Bull, are listed as being of special architectural and historic interest. Just opposite the ancient Village Institute is the village pump, now grandly roofed and pillared as a memento of days gone by.

⌘ WOOLVERSTONE

William Berners had already left his name upon a London street when he came to settle in Woolverstone. It was a happy choice, for of the many mansions built in the 18th century, few can have been more feliciously situated. Woolverstone lies on the quiet peninsula between the Orwell and the Stour, a few miles from the sea and not far from what is termed 'Constable country'. There were 400 acres of parkland, well-wooded and stocked with spotted deer. In front of the Hall the grounds slope down to the foreshore of the Orwell and there are splendid views from the Hall of the estuary and of the Nacton shore opposite, where another great house, Orwell Park, can be seen.

The Hall is beautifully proportioned and spacious with extensive wings to the main edifice connected by colonnades. It is built of Woolpit brick and is impressive with Ionic columns. The Berners are remembered by an obelisk set up in the park. William and his wife both died in the same year and their son Charles erected this monument, almost 100 feet high, in 1793. Also in the park is the handsome little church of St Michael, restored by Sir Gilbert Scott in 1832. Stone monkeys have always guarded the gateway to the park and also the almshouses nearby, built by the Berners. They are believed to have had some special significance for the Berners family since the monkey is incorporated into their crest.

Another animal mentioned here is the cat belonging to the Cat House, whose painted walls and white figure of a cat on the window-sill looks somewhat strange in this rural spot. The house was a haunt of smugglers, according to local tradition, and the white cat a signal to the shore.

At the end of the last war the Hall came into the possession of London County Council, whose original idea was to transfer the London Nautical School here for the benefit of boys of exceptional promise. It is now a boarding school for boys from London boroughs.

⌘ WORTHAM

The Wortham of the 19th century is clearly illuminated for us by the keen eyes and kindly judgment of the Rev Richard Cobbold, rector here for 52 years. The rector was of a literary turn of mind and published many poems and other works, including the Suffolk classic, *Margaret Catchpole*.

Cobbold came to the village with a heavy heart, as he admits to being unwilling to leave the cosy social round in Ipswich where he had been curate at St Mary-le-Tower, but there was no gainsaying the wishes of the bishop. Fortunately, the mood of despair soon changed and he became absorbed in the real needs of the parish while his prevailing relaxation was to record in words and sketches all the features and characters of the village that he came to love. There was not one cottager so slight or unimportant that he did not become a character in Cobbold's gallery.

An odd situation arose in 1830 in connection with the Dolphin Inn, so exactly on the border with Burgate that when beating the bounds it was usual to follow the line into the front door and out of the back. A boy of 13 had lived at the Dolphin for a time and on becoming a pauper presented the Poor Law Officers with a poser as to whether he was the responsibility of Wortham or Burgate. The bedroom he had

One of Wortham's attractive cottages

slept in was situated across the border line and it was decided that it all depended on the position of the bed. Here again there was a problem for the bed had been over the very beam that indicated the boundary. Calculations eventually revealed that the boy had been 5 inches in Wortham and the rest of him in Burgate.

One might expect from this that the onus of charity fell upon Burgate but when the case was presented it was decided that the pauper had no claim upon either parish because he had not been fully in one or the other.

⌘ YAXLEY

A very handsome and substantial village sign greets the visitor to Yaxley, close to the old Roman road between Ipswich and Norwich. The sign depicts a bird against a leafy background and apparently perching on a large wheel. It seems a bit of a puzzle. A few enquiries reveal that the bird is a cuckoo and is displayed because that is believed to be the meaning of the name Yaxley. The circle is a 'sexton's wheel' and even the most erudite may be forgiven for looking blank at this information since, apart from one at Long Stratton at the Norfolk end of the same road, Yaxley has the only one in the country.

A description of the 'sexton's wheel', believed to be of the 15th century, says that it consists of two wheels which are 2 feet 8 inches in diameter, revolving on the same axle. The wheels are marked with the six days sacred to the Blessed Virgin and at each of these points is a small hole to which a short piece of string is attached. 'Whenever a devout person was desirous of keeping a penance by fasting, he applied to the sexton to set the wheels spinning and whichever string he caught decided the day to begin the fast.'

Many theories were advanced about its use, including the idea that the wheels were merely for ornamenting church doors. However, some verses were discovered which promised to show some light, as in the lines:

> 'The Sexton turns the wheel about and bids the stander-by
> To hold the thread whereby he doth, the time and season try.'

⌘ YOXFORD

Travellers on the old Roman road from central Suffolk to the coast join up with the main A12 to Lowestoft and beyond in the middle of Yoxford. The village hugs the

Yoxford

junction, with most of the houses lining the approach road along the valley of the river Yox (which becomes the Minsmere at neighbouring Middleton).

No doubt with some reason the village gained the title of 'The Garden of Suffolk' at some time in the past. It may be that it refers to the gardens of the great houses here for there are three mansions with extensive grounds. In earlier days they must have absorbed the labour of most of the village. There is Grove Park, well named for its setting among trees on the south side, while the Rookery or Rookery Park has been justly proud of its gardens framed in ancient yew hedges. Cockfield Hall, a mansion of Tudor origin with much restoration, is Yoxford's direct association with a great event of history.

Here was kept under close guard by order of Queen Elizabeth herself, Katherine the unhappy sister of Lady Jane Grey, the Nine Days Queen. Lady Katherine Grey, married on the same day as her sister, had already suffered the pain of being deserted by her first husband and separated from her second. She spent the rest of her life at Cockfield Hall, was buried in the parish church but later removed to the more august precincts of Salisbury Cathedral.

At the peak of Yoxford's prosperity around 1869 when its population had increased from 800 in 1801 to about 1,300, a gazetteer gave this description of the village: 'It is situated in a remarkably pleasant neighbourhood, surrounded by beautiful country, interspersed with many seats of the gentry and is lighted by gas.' Of such things is the village story made.